If She Is Raped

Third Edition

Alan W. McEvoy and Jeff B. Brookings

Learning Publications, Inc.
Holmes Beach, Florida

ISBN 1-55691-199-8

Learning Publications, Inc.
5351 Gulf Drive
P. O. Box 1338
Holmes Beach, FL 34218-1338

Printing: 5 4 3 2 1   Year: 05 04 03 02 01

Printed in the United States of America

Contents

Acknowledgments

We wish to express our deepest appreciation to the many people who work with rape survivors and their families. Our conversations with them have generated many of the insights we share in the following pages. It is to these helpers, whose compassion and tireless efforts make such a positive difference, that this book is dedicated.

Dedication

With love to Allison, Cindy, Katy, Kyle, Ellie, Riley, and Sarah.

1
Understanding Rape

Rape is like a violent storm that cuts a swath through the lives of victims* and those who love them. Left in its wake are charged feelings of grief, anger, confusion, fear, helplessness, isolation, uncertainty, injustice, and a profound sense that one's world may never again be the same.

For many victims, rape is a defining moment that becomes a sharp divide in their lives . . . life before the rape and life now. In some measure, the same is true for those who are closest to the victim including husbands, fathers, brothers, and male companions. For all, one consequence of rape is that it can be a force that shapes peoples' perceptions of

---

*Rape experts use the words "victim" and "survivor" to describe a person who has been sexually assaulted. Generally speaking, a "victim" is one who suffers severe physical or mental injury as a result of an action by another person. A "survivor" is a person who lives beyond a traumatic event. The term "survivor" implies that a person has achieved a state of recovery from the trauma, whereas "victim" suggests that the person who has been harmed is still struggling to recover. In a sense, a victim of rape remains a victim until she decides to cease being a victim and is able to move her life beyond this violent event. This book attends to the needs of female victims who are on their way to becoming survivors.

themselves and their interactions with others. It seems as if many of the rules that governed how victims and their loved ones conducted their lives and related to one another are changed in the aftermath of rape.

Who we are as humans is embedded in our relationships with one another and in our capacity to choose our course of action. Rape harms both of these elemental human conditions. Rape alters the character of our bonds with one another, and often it removes from the victim a sense of agency . . . a sense that she can act on the world and not merely be acted upon. This form of violence makes the victim an object that is acted upon against her will according to the rapist's whim. As a result, the bonds that sustained the victim's sense of connectedness to others and her sense of agency are fundamentally altered.

How does a victim of rape regain control of her life? As a man who loves her, what can you do to help her recover? What obstacles must be confronted? How can you preserve and strengthen a relationship with someone you love if she is raped? To answer these questions, you must first understand what rape is.

Rape is an act of sexual violence that is usually perpetrated by males against females, which is accompanied by threat and intimidation, and which is imposed upon a victim against her will. Rape is about power, control, and domination. Rape should not be viewed as a form of sex, but as a violent crime that is expressed sexually. The victim has not "asked for it" and does not enjoy it. The victim was forced against her will by someone who overpowered her, and possibly terrorized her with a weapon and threats of bodily harm. Rape is life-threatening and life-altering; it severely traumatizes the victim.

Rape and attempted rape are disturbingly frequent crimes that occur thousands of times each year. Rape remains one of the least reported crimes, in part because many victims fear how they might be treated if they divulge what has happened to them. By choosing to remain silent, many rape survivors are also trying to protect others from the consequences of their victimization. It is an act of courage and trust for a woman to reveal to another that she was raped.

Fortunately, in recent years we have learned much about ways to help a rape victim. Understandably, most of the resources of community rape-crisis centers and counseling facilities are directed toward providing immediate assistance to the victim. But others also are in a position to help, including men. Because of the sexually violent nature of rape, however, males who are close to a victim may have a particularly difficult time coming to terms with what has happened. Our experience is that the husbands, fathers, brothers, and male partners of rape survivors are well-intentioned and want to help, but may not know what to do. Yet these males often have the greatest impact on her recovery—positively or negatively—depending on what they say and how they act.

Although most males want to help a loved one if she is sexually assaulted, many are ill-prepared to respond constructively. Perhaps this is because some males think of rape as a "woman's problem." They have little understanding of how rape can affect their relationship. To make matters worse, cultural myths and misunderstandings about rape compound the difficulties of recovery for victims. As a consequence, many well-intentioned men simply do not know what to do, or worse, they respond inappropriately to the recovery needs of the women they love.

Facts and Myths About Rape

There is no such thing as a "typical" rape or rape victim. Each episode is a unique and terrifying experience from which it requires time for the survivor to recover. There are, however, common elements and misconceptions associated with rape; awareness of them will help you to understand what she has been through.

To begin, rape is not the same as "making love." Although the majority of completed rapes involve vaginal penetration, this occurs in a state of emotional terror without the woman's consent. It is a complete misconception to believe the women "secretly desire" to be raped or taken by force. Victims *never* seek this terrible experience. Rape is a total violation of a woman's rights over her own body and of her ability to make a sexual choice. Rape is an attack not only on a woman's body, but on her sense of who she is and how she functions in the world. Indeed, from the woman's point of view, the sexual dimension of rape usually assumes lesser importance than the violent and dehumanizing aspects.

Rape is fundamentally an act of violence that may involve threats of bodily harm, extortion, deception, or subtle forms of manipulation designed to control the victim. Often the woman suffers severe physical injury. Rapists may use weapons or threats of violence to overpower their victims. Some rapists use drugs such as Rohypnol or GHB to incapacitate their victims and to impair their memories of the assault. Threats of violence may be accompanied by degrading verbal abuse. Any implication that the woman "asked for" or enjoyed the experience, or that rape and making love are the same, is a basic misconception. Even in the context of a friendly or dating relationship—a situation where large numbers of rapes occur—the rape still represents a violent assault and is not something the victim wants or enjoys. It is never appropriate to suggest that a woman somehow deserves to be assaulted.

A related fact is that the woman absolutely is not responsible for her victimization. Some men mistakenly assume that she could have prevented the rape by avoiding certain social situations, by dressing differently, or by putting up a fight. This mistaken assumption is even more likely if the victim exhibits no visible injuries. In fact, some males incorrectly believe that if she did not actively resist the attack, she must have given implied consent. Such a belief unfairly suggests that she is responsible for the assault.

Consent is never implied, nor should it ever be assumed. Consent means that both parties are equally free to act without fear, threat, or coercion. Consent means that one is not only able to freely choose, but also fully conscious in making a choice. A rapist does not offer his victim a choice. By its very definition, rape is a *nonconsensual* act. *Submitting* out of fear, or being *incapacitated* as a result of drugs or alcohol, means that consent is absent. A woman need not offer physical resistance for the encounter to be nonconsensual. Being paralyzed by fear or recognizing the futility of resistance in the face of threat does not make it consensual.

Believing that she is partially responsible only places emotional distance between the two of you at a time when your support is most needed. This causes her to have unnecessary feelings of guilt, anger and isolation. Blaming her hinders her recovery, and it could destroy your relationship.

Rape can occur at all hours of the day or night and in virtually any setting, including one's own home or a public place. Rape can happen to anyone, regardless of age, income, appearance or personal reputation. Although the majority of rape victims are single women between the ages of 12 and 24, there is no way to predict which women will be targeted by rapists. One common element is that rape is a frightening and degrading experience that requires time for victims to recover.

How You Can Help

Although there is no easy path to recovery from rape, you can help her by:

- **understanding** her fears and concerns
- **communicating** that she has the inner strength to overcome this adversity
- **knowing** how she and others may respond to the rape
- **demonstrating** compassion and acceptance
- **encouraging** her to make decisions which help her to regain control over her life

- **treating** her emotional state as understandable responses to the assault
- **helping** her prepare for what lies ahead
- **seeking** help and counseling for yourself
- **sharing** your feelings with her so that she knows she is not alone, that she has your unconditional love, and that this is a crisis you will endure together.

Remember, rape is a violent crime that is neither sought nor caused by the victim. Helping her to recover should be your chief concern.

Findings From the National Violence Against Women Survey

Experts have long recognized the limitations of statistical information about rape from traditional sources such as the Uniform Crime Reports and the National Crime Victimization Survey. Under-reporting of rape is common. In order to provide a more accurate picture of the prevalence (number of victims) and incidence (number of separate victimizations) of rape against women, the U.S. Department of Justice and the Centers for Disease Control and Prevention collaborated in sponsoring a state-of-the-art study. In a national random sample from 50 states and the District of Columbia, 8,000 adult women were interviewed about their experience of attempted and completed rape during their life. Rape was defined as "an event that occurred without the victim's consent, that involved the use or threat of force to penetrate the victim's vagina or anus by penis, tongue, fingers, or object, or the victim's mouth by penis." Researchers Patricia Tjaden and Nancy Thoennes published their comprehensive findings in November, 2000. The following are selected findings from the Full Report of the Prevalence, Incidence, and Consequences of Violence Against Women, published by the U.S. Department of Justice, Office of Justice Programs.

- 17.6 percent of all women (1 out of 6) are the victims of a completed or attempted rape at some time in their life

- over 300,000 women are forcibly raped each year in the United States; this figure does not include rapes against children and adolescents, and rapes against persons who are homeless or living in institutions

- 21.6 percent of female rape victims were younger than age 12 when they were first raped, and 32.4 percent were ages 12 to 17; thus, 54 percent were under age 18 when they experienced their first attempted or completed rape

- 8.1 percent of women reported being stalked at some time in their life; approximately 1 million women are stalked annually in the United States

- 41.4 percent of women who were raped since age 18 were also physically assaulted during the rape; only 35.6 percent of females who were physically injured during their most recent rape received medical treatment

- the majority of women surveyed were raped by a current or former intimate partner, a relative, or an acquaintance; 14.3 percent were raped by strangers

- multiple victimizations are relatively common; females who were raped as minors were twice as likely to be raped again as adults

2
Addressing Immediate Concerns

The time immediately following a rape is emotionally charged, confusing, and extremely anxious for the victim and for those who are close to her. Not only has she been terrorized and violated, but she now is faced with many additional worries. For example, directly following the rape, victims typically consider such questions as:

- Am I safe now?
- Do I need medical attention?
- Do I report this to the police?
- Am I pregnant?
- Did I contract a sexually transmitted infection such as syphilis or HIV?
- Should I tell my family and friends?
- What will I do when others find out?
- What will others think of me?
- How will this affect those I love?
- How does this affect my sexuality?

- Will he attempt to rape me again?
- Will my life ever be normal again?

The emotional consequences of rape continue well beyond the attack. Unfortunately, medical and legal professionals may unintentionally contribute to her trauma as they conduct their routines. For example, if the victim decides to immediately report the rape to the police, she is required to undergo an invasive medical exam *before* she changes clothes, bathes, eats, drinks, smokes, and if possible, before she urinates or defecates.*

Even if she chooses not to call the police, she still should be examined by a physicians soon as possible. First, she may require immediate medical attention. In addition, if she changes her mind and decides to report the rape, medical evidence will strengthen her case against the rapist. Finally, because sexually transmitted diseases have an incubation period, she will need to return to the physician approximately three weeks after the rape for follow-up tests.

Assisting her in receiving medical attention conveys the message that you believe her account and that you view her assault seriously. You are therefore communicating a powerful message of concern and support by letting her know that you are in this together and that this is not something she must face alone.

In the process of providing evidence to the police, she may have to recount the rape several times

---

*Because physical evidence does not stay viable for long, rape exams should be conducted as soon as possible (ideally within 24 hours of the attack). If a rape victim is unsure about reporting the crime, tell her that it is better to have medical evidence in case she later decides to inform the police.

in detail to strangers (usually men). She may be required to examine "mug" shots or help construct composite sketches of the rapist if his identity is not known to her. In some cases, police ask the victim to submit to a polygraph exam. Unfortunately, a police request to take a "lie detector test" unintentionally communicates the message that the police do not believe her report of being raped. Similarly, they may not take her story seriously if the test results are ambiguous.

The victim has every right to refuse to take a polygraph test and still expect her reported assault to be taken seriously. Lie detectors should not be used to determine a rape victim's credibility. Fortunately, most police investigators recognize this and seek to obtain evidence from the victim by other means. However, she may also request to take the test in order to further establish the credibility of her story.

Although it is true that rules of evidence require detailed questioning by police and prosecutors, these procedures may appear to her as an invasion of privacy. She may be especially reluctant to discuss certain elements of the rape such as anal penetration or being forced to perform oral sex. Such reluctance is rooted in feelings of shame, not lack of cooperation. At the very moment she most needs sympathetic understanding, impersonal routines can add to an already heavy emotional burden.

The time immediately following the rape requires from you understanding and compassion because the psychological forces contributing to her recovery are now in motion. How and what you communicate to her will affect how she feels about herself, her relationships, and her future. By what you say and do, you have the power to help her recover.

What You Should Do

In the immediate aftermath of rape, victims need gentleness and acceptance. To positively affect her recovery, there are things you should and should not do.

- A common initial reaction among men is an intense anger and a strong desire to seek revenge against the rapist. This is normal and understandable. Yet, this is a time when calm and reasoned judgments are most needed. It is especially important that *you do not contact the rapist,* even if his identity is known to you. Contact can create legal problems for you and cause the woman to fear for your safety. Threatening to take the law into your own hands adds unnecessarily to her emotional burden.

- Threatening the rapist is undesirable for other reasons as well. Your anger and threats of revenge shift attention away from her needs to yours. At a time when she most needs nurturance and understanding, the focus may become your anger rather than her recovery needs. Moreover, your anger can cut off communication; she may feel unable to talk about the incident because she does not wish to upset you. She may even feel guilty for "imposing" such an emotional burden on you. Finally, threatening revenge may cause her to fear you because your feelings of rage add a measure of unpredictability to the relationship. Letting your anger dominate only closes the lines of communication and reduces her sense of stability.

- Your anger should never be directed toward her. Under no circumstances should you accuse her or judge her. It is important for you to remain calm and to give her the opportunity, if she desires, to discuss the experience on her terms when she is ready.

- Reassure her that she is not responsible for being raped. Tell her that the attack was not caused by bad judgment or provocative behavior on her part. Do not ask her questions such as "Why didn't you scream and run? Why were you at that place at that time? Why did you talk to him in the first place?" Such "why" questions convey a sense of being judgmental, and may make her feel guilty and possibly resentful toward you. She needs to know that you do not blame her for failing to resist the rapist or for being in a situation that resulted in rape.

- Never imply that she secretly may have enjoyed the experience. Again, rape is a violent act that is not a source of pleasure for the victim. It is important for her to know that you do not equate her rape with an act of infidelity or promiscuity, and that you do not see her as defiled or less moral than prior to the incident.

- Just as many males accept as true some of the myths and stereotypes about rape, so too do many women. When she is ready, encourage her to discuss any beliefs or myths about rape which may contribute to her emotional state. Tell her that you do not accept views that blame the woman. Help her to put the blame where it belongs . . . on the perpetrator. Always let her know that you believe her, even if others have doubts. To doubt her version of events is to undermine her ability to share feelings with you.

- Rape robs the woman of a sense of control over her life. In order for her to regain this sense of control, she should be encouraged to make decisions about all events affecting her life (e.g., whether to report the crime, go to trial, tell family and friends, seek counseling). Do not make these decisions for her or demand that she follow a particular course of action, even though you want to help her by "taking charge." You are not "in charge" of her recovery . . . she is. It is important for you to communicate your unfailing support for her in the decisions *she* makes.

- Do not demand of her immediate, open communication about the rape. She may not have had sufficient time to sort out her feelings, or she may wish to hide her feelings due to a deep-seated sense of embarrassment. It is particularly important that you refrain from unintentionally humiliating her by prying into the sexually intimate aspects of the rape. Allow her the freedom to discuss such issues when she is ready.

Because her world seems in turmoil, your loved one needs to feel that she is not alone and that you will endure this crisis *together*. Regardless of what happened, she should know that your love for her remains intact.

3
Communicating with the Victim

Discussing the assault can be a major source of anxiety for the rape victim, yet effective communication is important to her long-term adjustment and to the survival of her valued relationships. Unfortunately, many relationships end or undergo severe strain in the aftermath of an assault. Communication often is disrupted, people may feel frustrated and helpless, and anger or resentment toward loved ones may erupt. Given the emotional turmoil you both are experiencing, there are several ways to promote effective communication.

- Be patient, approachable, and show that you accept her unconditionally. By giving her the opportunity to express feelings at a pace that is comfortable to her, you will help her work through emotional conflicts and you will gain a better understanding of her needs.

- Do not pressure or "interrogate" her by insisting that she recount the details of the incident repeatedly. When she is ready to discuss the rape and her feelings about it,

she will do so. Forcing her to be candid may
make her resent you.

- You should never express anger toward her
  if she initially is reluctant to talk, or if she
  delays telling you for a period of time. Do
  not accuse her of "hiding something" because she did not tell you sooner. Many victims protect loved ones from the pain and
  turmoil caused by the revelation of being
  raped. She may also fear being blamed or rejected. Her prolonged silence should not be
  interpreted as a rejection of you, but as her
  way of sorting things out.

- Tell her that it is understandable if she is
  fearful. Rapists often threaten to seriously
  harm their victims if they do not comply or if
  they tell anyone what happened. Talking
  about fear can be a positive step toward
  overcoming it.

- Do not tell her you know how she feels. Only
  she truly knows. Also, do not tell her "everything is all right" when everything is *not* all
  right.

- Pay special attention to recurring themes in
  her conversations. These might be clues providing insight into issues which are especially troublesome to her. Being raped can
  bring out much "unfinished business" that
  has long troubled her, including problems
  which may already exist in her relationship
  with you. By being alert to her conversa-
  tional themes and by being open to discuss
  sensitive issues, you will come to better un-

derstand her trauma and help her to resolve painful issues.

- Eventually, it is important for the two of you to discuss the impact of the rape on your relationship. The emotional consequences of rape are traumatic for all those involved with the victim, especially you. Calmly sharing your feelings and your vulnerabilities with her will promote the mutual nurturing that aids the recovery process.

- Consider relationship counseling. Many rape crisis centers provide such services at little or no cost. A competent, sensitive therapist can help remove barriers to effective communication.

Remember that no single response is typical of all women who have been raped. One challenge for you is to avoid being drawn into conflicts that are rooted in her emotional turmoil. Whether it is her silence, mood swings, anger, or feelings of fear and helplessness, remain constant in your love and support.

What to Say to Others

Close friends and family members frequently respond in ways that mirror the victim: shock, denial, rage, confusion, guilt, and helplessness. Such reactions are rooted in efforts to make sense out of a cruel and senseless event. Although it is important for others to express their feelings and to demonstrate their concern and support, sometimes well-intentioned efforts are based on misconceptions about rape and can create additional emotional burdens for

her. You can help by serving as a "buffer" between
the victim and others. The following hints will help.

- Family members and friends may seek to al-
  leviate their own feelings of helplessness by
  threatening revenge against the rapist.
  Again, such threats may further traumatize
  her and cause her to worry about the safety
  of those close to her. Threats also complicate
  her dealings with law enforcement. Their
  anger can be expressed to you or a counselor,
  but not to the victims. Such expressions of
  anger may heighten her anxiety and make
  her feel guilty.

- Discourage others from trying to lift her spirits
  by joking about the assault. Jokes trivialize the
  rape and are likely to confuse and isolate her
  rather than being a means of raising her spirits.

- Respect the victim's wishes for confidentiality. She should decide what information
  should be divulged to whom. Also, you
  should not prevent her from talking to others if she chooses.

- Well-intentioned family members may try to
  solicit support from close friends, clergy, co-
  workers and others without the victim's permission. Such efforts to intervene, unless
  she requests them, should be discouraged.

- Empower the victim; do not try to control or
  overprotect her. Some may seek to convince
  her to change dwellings or accept what
  amounts to 24-hour surveillance. These actions may reinforce the woman's view of herself as vulnerable and powerless, thus

discouraging her from mobilizing her own resources for coping. This can promote an unhealthy dependency on others . . . a dependency that may come to be resented. Providing support should not function to increase feelings that she has lost control over her life or that she is no longer self-reliant. Being supportive means helping her to build self-confidence and independence.

- Let her decide when a distraction is appropriate and necessary. She will not recover sooner simply because there is a "friendly conspiracy" to keep her mind off the incident. Occupying her time with a variety of activities and acting as if the rape never happened may communicate to her that the assault is too shameful to discuss or acknowledge. There will be times when she wants to engage in certain activities, but it should be at her request.

- Remind family and friends that she has privacy needs. At times it is desirable and therapeutic for her to work through feelings alone. Sometimes a constant stream of well-wishers will be an emotional drain. It is especially difficult for her to put the incident behind her if she feels obliged to satisfy the frequent inquiries of visitors about "what happened" and "how are you doing?" When she decides she needs to be alone, respect that decision. In addition, she may want you to communicate such decisions to others for her. In doing so, you will assure family and friends that their concern is recognized and appreciated. In respecting her wish for privacy, you will send two empowering messages: she is the best judge of what she needs, and she has the inner strength to recover.

- Remind others never to imply that the attack was caused because of what she did or failed to do. Such second-guessing is a form of "victim blaming" that complicates her recovery. This is especially true in the case of teenagers who are victimized in the context of dating. Avoid suggesting that her action, rather than the behavior of the rapist, is at fault.

Clearly, one of the chief tasks you face is to work with the victim's loved ones to provide a safe, accepting climate for her to release painful feelings without fear of criticism. By letting her know that you trust her ability to recover, you help empower her to reclaim her life.

4
Responding to Long-Term Consequences

The consequences of rape often linger far beyond the attack and its immediate aftermath. Rape can be an all-consuming experience for a survivor; it may dominate her thoughts and cast a dark emotional shroud over her life. If you think of rape as a profoundly violent physical and psychological invasion that destroys a victim's equilibrium, you can understand why it may take months or years for her to come to terms with its residual effects.

Although no two survivors of rape necessarily go through the same sequence of experiences as they struggle to recover, there are common elements in the recovery process. One of the long-term consequences of rape has its origins in what happens immediately before the rape. Victims of rape commonly experience preimpact terror. This refers to the very frightening moments just prior to the assault, when the victim knows what is about to happen but is powerless to stop it.

The courts recognize preimpact terror as a legitimate aspect of injury. In civil court, for example, special damages can be awarded to the families of airplane-crash victims for the period of time the passengers know the plane is going to crash . . . until it does. These damages are based upon the emotional injuries associated with the extreme terror experienced when passengers realize that a crash is imminent. The same principle applies to rape victims. What some victims report experiencing during the moments before the attack is an intense wave of almost simultaneous conflicting thoughts and emotions—denial, disbelief, indecision, injustice, intense fear, disorientation, defeat. At the heart of preimpact terror is the realization that there is no escape, that one will be intentionally harmed, and that one may never be the same again.

The reason why an understanding of preimpact terror is important to a victim's recovery has to do with how she may mentally reconstruct the rape. She is likely to relive the moments before the attack and second guess herself because she was unable to stop what was happening. A victim's feelings of guilt, shame, self-blame, and self-doubt often can be linked to the second guessing of decisions she made as the rape unfolded. Although she may have been frightened for her life, in reliving the event, she imposes upon herself an unreasonable standard of conduct based upon guilt-ridden speculation about how she should have acted. However logical or reasonable such a standard of conduct may seem in retrospect now that she is safe, you should help her to understand that as the assault progressed, she was in a state of terror as she was overwhelmed by the rapist.

Is it reasonable to think logically under such circumstances? She bears no blame.

Rape-related Post-traumatic Stress Disorder

For many years, rape crisis counselors described the psychological and behavioral effects of sexual assault as the "Rape Trauma Syndrome." This "syndrome" was not viewed as a mental disorder, but as a series of stages that many victims of rape go through during the recovery process. Today, the dominate clinical model views the post-assault reactions of rape survivors as reflecting Rape-related Post-traumatic Stress Disorder (RR-PTSD), which results from the survivor's attempts to cope with feelings of helplessness and vulnerability caused by the rape. Perhaps as many as one third of rape victims show signs of RR-PTSD, which include the following major symptoms.

1. ***Intrusive, uncontrolled thoughts about the rape.*** These may take the form of dreams, recurring nightmares, and graphic flashbacks that seem to "pop" into the victim's head at any time. Most distressing about these thoughts, particularly the flashbacks, is that they are experienced not merely as recollections, but almost as if the rape is happening now and the victim is reliving the trauma. Sometimes these flashbacks involve vivid sexual imagery but are not like the sexual fantasies that most people experience. One important difference is that fantasies are pleasurable and flashbacks are not. Another difference between

fantasies and flashbacks is that a person can control a fantasy. A flashback, however, seems to control the victim. The mental image that is triggered intrudes itself upon the victim despite her wishes to make it stop. Accompanying the flashback may be physical reactions such as uncontrollable shaking, chills, heart palpitations, or nausea.

2. ***Avoidance of reminders.*** Certain sights, sounds, smells, activities, places, or other cues that correspond to the rape can trigger in victims unwanted thoughts. Many will go to great lengths to avoid such reminders, possibly extending their avoidance behavior to people, places, activities, or other things that may be only remotely related to the assault. This strategy can be self-defeating because among the eliminated activities may be some that previously had been a source of pleasure and relaxation.

3. ***Hyper-vigilance and arousal.*** In the aftermath of rape, many victims are in a constant state of high alert for possible danger. It is as if they are always on guard and cannot seem to let their guard down. This hyper-vigilance in relation to every sight and sound in the environment is mentally and emotionally draining. As a consequence, many rape victims experience fatigue, irritability, lapses of concentration, exaggerated startle responses, and sleep deprivation.

4. ***Social withdrawal.*** In an effort to avoid feeling pain, many victims simply withdraw from social contacts. This can include being "disconnected" from loved ones who are a natural source of support. It is as if these victims place a shell around themselves so that they can avoid feeling anything . . . and nothing and no one can get to them. Such social withdrawal often manifests itself in a persistent state of flattened affect where the victim displays little emotion. Accompanying this withdrawal is usually very low self-esteem, depression, and possibly thoughts of suicide.

The National Organization for Victim Assistance website provides examples of "trigger" events that remind the victim of the assault. Such disturbing reminders may include the following.

- Seeing or hearing about the assailant.
- Sensing (e.g., seeing, hearing, smelling) something similar to elements present during the assault.
- Reading or watching news accounts of the event or similar incidents.
- "Anniversaries" of the assault.
- Proximity of the anniversary of the attack to holidays, birthdays, or other significant life events.
- Critical phases of criminal or civil proceedings.

Other Rape Trauma Reactions

We stress again that no two rape survivors necessarily react the same way. Not every survivor will
exhibit symptoms of Rape-related Post-traumatic
Stress Disorder. A victim's responses following rape
reflect her prior experiences (especially her experience with trauma), her personality, the character of
her support system, and any other combination of
variables. Nevertheless, there are some common elements or "phases" that are typical as she struggles
to recover.

The immediate impact of rape usually produces
acute distress in victims. This may include shock,
disbelief, confusion, fear, anxiety, crying, humiliation, embarrassment, self-blame, and other signs of
emotional disorganization. She may even appear extremely controlled on the surface, masking more
troubling emotions at a deeper level. (Ironically, if
the woman remains stoic, police officers and others
may doubt that she was raped. Such doubts only add
to her distress.) At the same time, a number of
physical symptoms may appear such as soreness and
bruising from the attack, vaginal or rectal bleeding,
tension headaches, fatigue, sleep disturbances, nausea, and lack of appetite.

As part of the immediate impact phase, abrupt
changes in mood are common. To compound her distress, she may feel that she is overreacting to normal
everyday concerns and become upset with herself.
She may appear to be on an emotional roller coaster
that seems to border on extremes—sometimes near
rage, sometimes in tears.

During this time, it is important for you to remember that her physical and emotional reactions

are normal responses to a terrifying, life-threatening experience. Her reactions may also be complicated by the inappropriate responses of others to her rape. If she exhibits these symptoms, let her know that her feelings and behaviors are understandable, and that such reactions do not mean that she is "going crazy."

Gradually, the victim enters a period of apparent readjustment. During this phase, she may announce that the incident has been forgotten and give every indication that it is no longer troubling. Her resoluteness may appear to be a sign of full recovery, but, typically, it is not. If anything, the assault lingers in the background of her thoughts, even though she may openly deny that it continues to bother her. In part, denial is intended to protect others from her turmoil. It is also important to understand that such denial is not an indication of deception or stubbornness on her part. Neither is it self-destructive. Instead, denial allows her to control the pace of her recovery so that she will not be overwhelmed by an onslaught of images and emotions.

Eventually, the victim may experience a seemingly abrupt re-emergence of assault-related memories. It may appear that she has relapsed and is getting worse rather than better. Although this can be very disturbing to her and to those close to her, she may in fact be moving toward integration. It is as if she has given herself permission to think about these troubling memories because she is now in a better position to cope emotionally and to reorganize her life. The initial sign of integration can be a return of the troubling responses that she may have experienced earlier (e.g., nightmares, insomnia, eat-ing disturbances, panic attacks, headaches). Some victims become so upset at this seeming relapse that they self-medicate with drugs or alcohol, or possibly have suicidal thoughts. These experiences, however, are largely an "echo" of her initial acute responses; usually they are not experienced with the same intensity or duration as before. Such responses, while understandably upsetting to all, may be seen as a not-so-silent announcement that she is beginning to meaningfully process and to integrate the images and feelings associated with the attack. Simply stated, she is coming to terms with what has happened so that she may get on with her life.

Many relationships undergo their greatest stress at this time because she appears to be getting worse. How well a victim copes during this period often reflects the strength of her support system. If she feels unsupported, she may externalize her distress through aggression, or internalize it through suicidal depression and shame. Your patience, understanding, and support here is critical.

Perhaps the most common denominator at the base of all aspects of the recovery process is a victim's feeling that she is somehow to blame for the rape and the turmoil it has caused. In order to help her deal with feelings of self-blame, you should convey to her the following simple truths.

- Regardless of where she was, how she was dressed, what she had been drinking, or toward whom she may have been friendly, she did not deserve to be raped and she did not cause the assault.

- She is not responsible for the behavior of the rapist or for what happens to him in the event of legal action.

- The fact that she survived the rape is what matters; her survival means that she did the right thing so she need not second guess herself.

- Those who love her, especially you, will remain supportive. She need not be ashamed or feel guilty if her victimization has temporarily upset those who care about her.

- She has the strength to regain control over her life and to move forward.

Coping with Grief

Grief is a natural response to personal loss which poses both challenges and opportunities. The challenges are especially complex if the grieving is due to being victimized by sexual assault. The initial shock following a rape often is replaced with an ill-defined but lingering feeling of grief among victims. This feeling of grief is due to the loss of one's sense of safety, trust, independence, and personal control.

The issue of grief recovery is particularly critical for husbands, fathers and male friends in their efforts to deal with loved ones in the aftermath of a rape. Rape victims are especially susceptible to the advice given to them by males whom they have come to trust. Unfortunately, much of the well-intentioned advice regarding how victims should and should not cope with rape reflects myth and folk wisdom rather than a sound understanding of the recovery process. Bad advice on how to cope is particularly worrisome because it can result in increased self-doubt. By understanding the myths and the process of grief recovery, males can be in a better position to offer practical suggestions to help loved ones.

Perhaps the most common misunderstanding regarding grief is that "time heals all wounds," and that time alone constitutes a magical potion which will somehow cover up deep feelings of loss. The problem is that simply "giving it time" does not necessarily resolve conflicts produced by the rape. To make matters worse, by telling a rape victim that only time will heal feelings of grief, you are unintentionally reinforcing feelings of powerlessness. Simply stated, it conveys the message that nothing you or anyone else does will relieve the emotional pain of rape, that she is ultimately alone in her suffering, and that inaction (i.e., waiting) rather than action is the only way to cope.

Another misconception is that she "shouldn't think about it" or "shouldn't feel that way." Implied here are several unfortunate messages. First, by telling the victim not to dwell on the rape, you are telling her to ignore or to bury powerful feelings. Suppressing or ignoring feelings does not produce a sense of resolution, nor does it result in an emotional state which will allow the woman to get on with her life. Second, by telling an assault survivor not to feel a certain way, you are denying her the right to her feelings. You are also implying that she is somehow inadequate for not rationally controlling her emotional state, even though that is not the message you intend to communicate.

Such messages produce three unfortunate consequences. First, the woman in a state of grief begins to experience guilt for feeling (or not feeling) a certain way. This only adds to feelings of self-blame. Second, the victim becomes very guarded in expressing to others how she truly feels out of fear of being judged, censored, or rejected. At a time when honest communication with loved ones is critical, the woman feels unable to talk about what she is going through. Finally, encouraging victims of rape to bury their emotions only serves to confuse them about their true feelings. Recovery from rape is accomplished when she feels free to be honest with herself and truly is in touch with her feelings. Denial, guilt, and an inability to share feelings with others is a recipe for prolonging the anguish and limiting growth potential.

There are two common bits of folk wisdom which encourage rape victims to deny or suppress their feelings. The first is to tell them to "keep busy." Immersion into work or other activities does not magically cause one in a state of grief to "snap out of it." Temporary distractions are just that . . . temporary; they often serve to avoid or prolong coming to terms with problems. Engaging in work, hobbies or other activities while grieving has value to a point, so long as it does not result in being isolated from sources of support or in denying her feelings. (The same is true when a person attempts to suppress grief by medicating himself or herself into oblivion.)

The second piece of folk wisdom suggests that one can diminish feelings of loss by acquiring something new. An example of this is telling a child whose pet has died "not to worry, you will be okay, we'll get you a new one." The obvious problem is that grief caused by rape is not offset by new possessions. Although well-intentioned, suggesting that something new will somehow result in recovery may be interpreted by her as trivializing her feelings. It may also be interpreted as a crass attempt to buy off her sense of grief and get her to act as if everything is back to normal. Little wonder that many victims of rape learn to act as if they have recovered, while continuing to suffer in silence.

The problem of "acting recovered" is especially common because the victim neither wants to burden others, nor does she want to feel rejected because others do not know how to respond to her. Both the victim and others may "put on a happy face" to avoid confronting true feelings. Because most people find it difficult to know how to respond to another's grief, it becomes a simple thing for all concerned to avoid the subject altogether. Complex feelings of denial, guilt, anger, confusion and fear are then compounded by this conspiracy of silence and the resulting sense of isolation.

Impact on Males

Males often pass through a series of phases similar to those of the victim. Included here are shock, confusion, intense anger, and feelings of guilt and self-blame for "failing to protect" a loved one. As a result, males also need to achieve resolution of the incident.

Many males whose loved ones have been raped feel a kind of "impotent rage"—wanting to strike out but having no appropriate means to do so. Your feelings of anger are a natural and common reaction. As we have already indicated, however, your feelings about the incident should be expressed to her in a gentle and calm manner, rather than in a state of extreme agitation or rage. This will keep the lines of communication open which is critical for the survival of your relationship with her.

Understanding and coping with anger is a key element in your mutual recovery. It is not uncommon for some of the intense anger men feel toward the rapist to be directed toward the victim. This transferring of anger is a gradual and subtle process, of which you may not even be aware. Directing anger toward the victim happens for a number of reasons, including the following.

- You may feel anger toward the victim because she has dependency needs which place additional demands on you. The turmoil caused by the incident taxes both of you emotionally, and it is likely that there are times when you may feel her need for understanding and patience is unrealistic or excessive. Ironically, oftentimes males initially encourage the victim to feel dependent on them, then later come to resent what they believe is her overdependence.

- You may feel that she is using her victimization as a means of manipulating you and others. Perhaps you feel that she is trying to draw attention to herself, to elicit pity, or to use the incident to avoid her responsibilities. If she does so, it is probably not an attempt to manipulate and control you; rather, it may be her way of regaining the sense of personal control that was taken away by her assailant.

- You may feel anger because her recovery is progressing slower than you would like. You may be frustrated because she does not seem to forget the incident and put it behind her. It is important to remember that people recover at different rates and in different ways. It is unrealistic and inappropriate for you to impose on her the terms of her recovery. Such an imposition communicates a lack of understanding and is likely to be a source of her feeling resentment toward you.

- As we mentioned earlier, some victims of sexual assault are reluctant to talk about what happened. Even though you feel that you are entitled to have her confide in you, her reluctance to discuss the incident should not incite you to anger. It does not mean that she is "hiding" something or that she does not trust you. Rather than being angry, you could indicate to her that it is acceptable for her to guard her feelings, and that you are ready to listen patiently whenever she is ready to talk.

- It is common for males to have revenge fantasies about getting even with the rapist. Harboring revenge fantasies does not mean that your fundamental nature is becoming more violent. These thoughts are normal and reflect your desire for justice, particularly if other means of legal redress are not available. Acting on such fantasies, however, is inappropriate and legally problematic. Although you should not let revenge fantasies dominate your communications with the victim, it is helpful to talk about such thoughts with a counselor or other person trained in rape recovery.

Working toward Recovery

Recovery from rape is something like taking "two steps forward, one step back." Recovery is not necessarily a discrete series of stages that all victims and their loved ones go through in a sequential manner. Rape victims often fluctuate dramatically between recovery phases. This can be frustrating and confusing because there is no simple way for either of you to deal with these complex feelings. To encourage her recovery, there are several things you should and should not do. The following suggestions will further build upon those mentioned earlier.

- Do not become angry if she *refuses* to accept help that you or others may offer. Constant offers of help, though well-intended, can seem like a burden. Similarly, do not demand that she "get help" as a condition for your continued support. She needs to decide the terms under which she accepts help. If she refuses counseling, you can secure helpful materials that she can read or view on her own. Most rape-crisis or counseling centers have such resources. If she finds this material to be of value, then she may be more willing to accept additional help.

- Because she cannot will herself to stop having troubling thoughts and feelings, do not tell her to "stop thinking about it." In gen-

eral, avoid using the word "should" in your
discussions with her.

- Do not express irritation or anger toward
  her if her recovery seems too slow. We cannot stress too strongly that rape victims recover at different rates and in a variety of
  ways. It will create conflict if you try to impose conditions on her recovery. Such an imposition communicates a lack of understanding, rather than compassion, and is
  likely to be a cause of resentment.

- Consider doing the kinds of joint activities
  that have brought you closer together in the
  past. For most rape victims, a sharp dividing
  line now exists between their pre-and post-
  assault memories. Engaging in joint activities gives both of you opportunities to redis-
  cover those positive, shared memories that
  form the preassault foundation of your relationship. Sharing positive activities helps to
  ensure that your relationship will endure
  the difficult times ahead.

- When it is appropriate and mutually agreed
  upon, seek the companionship of friends who
  are healthy and up-beat. The good cheer that
  you experience from being around positive
  people provides a needed respite for both of
  you.

- Do not act out in violent ways in the mistaken belief that violence is a good release
  for pent-up anger. Because she may recoil
  from anything or anyone associated with violence, such violence will only isolate her.
  Simply stated, violent outbursts harm the

relationship and are contrary to the recovery process.

- Do not rely on alcohol (or other drugs) to numb the pain and frustration. Substance abuse will almost certainly create further problems as you both struggle to cope.

- Do not assume that becoming a "workaholic" will make the recovery process easier of either of you. Although work can have therapeutic value to a point, excessive involvement in work may communicate to her that she assumes a back seat to other concerns.

- After the initial shock, some males become angry toward the victim for "allowing" the incident to occur. This is especially true in the case of fathers whose adolescent daughters have been assaulted in a dating situation. Even if she had been drinking or had used poor judgment, blaming her for being irresponsible will only cause her to be angry with you. Ultimately, conveying feelings of anger and blame will close off communication and hinder your relationship.

- Agreeing to pretend that the rape never happened does not end the anger. If anything, such a pretense promotes emotional dishonesty and poor communication. It is acceptable to be honest with yourself and with your loved one that anger about the incident is one of the feelings you are experiencing. Being emotionally honest is a sign of trust in the other and encourages honesty in return.

- Find a trusted person with whom *you* can talk without fear of being judged. For some, it is especially useful to locate support groups in which members meet regularly to discuss their experiences and strategies for healing. Knowing that others have endured what you are going through can provide hope.

Remember that each person has developed his or her own ways of coping with emotional stress. Share your feelings with each other but do not expect her methods of coping to be identical to yours. With mutual support and openness, you both will recover and you may succeed in building a relationship with her which is even stronger, because you endured a crisis *together*.*

---

*We strongly recommend that she read a companion volume to this book written for rape victims. The book is entitled *If You Are Raped*, 3rd ed. by Kathryn M. Johnson, Learning Publications, Inc., 2001.

5
Overcoming Fears about Sex

One significant consequence of rape is anxiety about sexual activity. For a young victim this may be her first "sexual" experience, causing her great confusion about human sexuality. For all victims, rape is done in a violent context devoid of love and emotional intimacy. Her being raped may result in a long-term fear of sexual involvement, a diminished sexual desire, a feeling that she has been rendered "asexual," or the rape may aggravate sexual difficulties that already existed between partners.

For men who are the sexual partners of rape victims, there is likely to be a temporary disruption of sexual activity. Difficulties may be especially acute if the rape was extremely violent, sadistic, or involved multiple rapists. Many victims experience changes in their sexual responsiveness, and are concerned about the responses of their partners.

It is not uncommon for a rape victim to experience flashbacks during consensual sexual relations. If you are insensitive to her needs, it may make the resumption of sex seem rape-like, reminding her of the incident. Likewise, males are often insecure about their sexual performance, especially if she seems reluctant or unresponsive. In other words, both partners normally experience complex feelings about sexual impulses following a rape. As her partner, you should ask yourself, "How can I effectively communicate with the woman I love when she has been sexually assaulted?" The following suggestions will help.

- She needs to be given every opportunity to regain her sense of personal control, especially in the area of sexual decision making. Do not demand or pressure her into sexual activity. Resuming sex is not necessarily a means of normalizing the relationship or of helping her to recover. A resumption of sexual activity may *seem* like a behavioral indicator that things are back to normal, even though they are not. It is as if one or both of you are saying, "See, we are having sex again, so things must be okay." Unless she is ready for the resumption of sex, the act of love-making may serve to diminish her sexual desires and complicate your relationship. Let her make sexual decisions, especially if she needs a period of abstinence.

- Do not be angry with her or doubt your adequacy if she appears less sexually responsive than before. It may be that certain cues present during the rape (e.g., the smell of alcohol) remind her of the assault and inhibit her responsiveness. A willingness to talk honestly about such troubling associations and to alter patterns will help your relationship.

- Just as you should not pressure her into an early resumption of sex, neither should you avoid any display of intimacy. Understandably, some males assume that victims will have a diminished interest in sex and they therefore emotionally withdraw from her. It is important that she does not misinterpret your behavior as a sign that you feel she is "tarnished" by the rape or less appealing than before. There are many ways to express intimacy (e.g., hugging; non-sexual massage) without consummating that intimacy sexually. For example, asking permission to hold or cuddle her is appropriate. Again, honest communication and a willingness to take your cues from her will help.

- Acknowledge that sexually graphic flashbacks and panic attacks do not mean that her capacity for a healthy sexual relationship is fundamentally changed. Reassure her that you understand the occurrence of flashbacks is a common but temporary consequence of rape. Encourage her to talk about those things that trigger a flashback, because identifying and talking about these triggers can reduce her vulnerability to them. Tell her that if she wishes, you will listen in a non-judgmental way to any flashback imagery she feels able to discuss.

- Some males experience erotic feelings when the victim describes the rape to them, and then feel guilty for having such feelings.

This merely demonstrates the fact that rape produces a variety of conflicting emotions in people. If you do feel aroused when learning of the incident, *do not* communicate these feelings to the victim because this will only provoke greater anxiety in her. If such feelings persist, it would be valuable to seek the assistance of a counselor.

- Be patient. Sexual disruption following rape usually is temporary and can be overcome with sensitivity and understanding. If problems persist, counseling can be helpful. An important step in gaining control over powerful and after conflicting feelings is to articulate them to someone who understands.

In a truly remarkable book entitled *Working With Available Light: A Family's World After Violence* (W. W. Norton and Co., Inc., 1999), author Jamie Kalven chronicles the aftermath of the brutal rape of his wife, Patsy, by a stranger. His accurate recording of their conversations over many months following the attack offers readers an eloquent and insightful account of the struggles he and Patsy endured. The book also chronicles the sustaining power of love and hope amidst a crisis. The following are selected quotes from the book in the words of both Patsy and Jamie.

Patsy

- *I feel as if I looked into a black hole. He (the rapist) dragged me to the edge, and I looked in. It was the place where torture victims and people in concentration camps are thrown like pieces of garbage.*

- *What was so unnerving . . . was the knowledge that of how quickly you can be ripped out of the world and isolated by violence.*

- *If I had been killed, this is what the children would have been left with—this photograph. . . . . It's hard for me to believe there was ever a time when I didn't have this thing inside me. . . . I'm not the person in that picture any more.*

- *I'm healed in all the outside ways, but I'm left with these terrible feelings. . . . When I run into someone I haven't seen for a long time, someone who doesn't know what happened, I feel as though I'm talking across a great distance. A part of me wants to say, "Don't you see, everything's changed. I'm a different person now."*

- *When we start to make love, I feel as if everything has been taken from me—my body, my freedom, and any possibility of pleasure. I feel I've been robbed . . . it's as if the wires inside me are crossed.*

- *I can see now how it works, how the feelings left by the attack become part of whatever is problematic in your life—your marriage, or sex, or whatever. It comes to be seen as who you are.*

- *I'm depressed about what's happened to my life. And I'm depressed about what I'm doing to your life.*

- *I don't think you understand the humiliation I continue to feel at not being able to be on my own—it includes running, going to meetings*

*at night, driving—general dependency. . . .
Every day has its own terrifying moment—
every night has its dream.*

- *Every day I consciously try to find one thing
  that makes me feel peaceful. I struggle to find
  this little connection here and that little connection there that might make me feel everything is going to be okay.*

Jamie

- *It was as if the attack provided an opening for
  others to acknowledge how frightened they
  were. Several women said, "If this can happen
  to Patsy . . . "—Patsy who is so strong and
  competent and experienced—then no one is
  safe. Again and again, in the faces of women
  friends I saw the same look of recognition:
  This thing I have always feared. . . . I was
  aware, too, of a distance that had opened between women and men: a man had done this
  to Patsy. And I was a man.*

- *I hated the idea that he—this faceless pro-
  noun—was now a presence in our lives and
  that she, in some sense, remained in his
  grasp.*

- *Patsy was inside something I was outside of.
  The assault had dislocated her from our
  shared life.*

- *During the first weeks after the assault, I
  took refuge in action. Yet there were also the
  moments- in-between. Most often they came
  when I was alone in the car. As I drove from
  here to there, through the streets of my life,*

grief would balloon inside me, and I would sob.

- *Patsy's recoil from me had been immediate; she could scarcely stand to be touched or kissed. It was as if she wanted to make love with me without touching her.*

- *I love the sight of her—her open face, her appetite for life, her generous stance in the world. But on intimate ground her body becomes stricken by fear. Like a porcupine curling into a bristling ball, she stubbornly withholds herself.*

- *Would we ever touch if I didn't do the touching? Sometimes I think what Patsy wants is for me to be present yet disembodied. She tolerates my touch but does not answer to it. I feel the resistance inside her seeming passivity, the reaction inside her inaction.*

- *She saw my confusion as evidence of my failure to understand her condition.*

- *I am beginning to see that when others fail to acknowledge the reality and gravity of what has happened, when their patterns of denial and evasion deepen the isolation of the victim, they compound the injury of the rape. It is indecent that the victim, as she struggles to fashion a narrative that moves the cruelties inflicted upon her from the interior regions of her soul into the world, must not only contend with the weight of her knowledge and the undertow of her shame but also with the counterforce of institutions and individuals who resist the telling of her story.*

- *My love for this woman, whom I have found
  so attractive, so frustrating, so compelling for
  so many years is like a vessel carrying me
  (forever en route, never arriving) toward the
  center of my life.*

A Special Word to Fathers

When the victim of sexual assault is a child or
adolescent, the emotional impact on her and her
family is especially severe. Fathers, who have a
strong sense of responsibility for the safety of their
daughters, may have particularly intense reactions
such as rage and self-blame. In the crucial hours and
days following the rape, however, it is absolutely
critical that you be aware of the stresses on your
child. The following should be kept in mind:

- Rape may have been your daughter's first
  sexual experience, causing her to have exaggerated fears about adult intimacy. Your
  daughter, regardless of her age, needs to
  know that she is not tarnished, that her capacity to have close relationships is not diminished, and that rape is not how loving
  couples express themselves sexually. She
  also needs to understand that rape is a crime
  of violence, not an act of "uncontrolled pas-
  sion," and that she bears no responsibility
  for the violence inflicted upon her.

- Research indicates that coerced sexual encounters, including forcible rape, are how a
  large number of young victims are first "initiated" into sex. Concerns over "loss of virginity" become an issue. A young victim, for
  example, may believe that she is no longer a

virgin because she was raped or sexually molested. She needs to understand that because she did not freely give herself to the assailant, and because the act was not consensual, her virginity is still intact.

- Because many fathers find it difficult to discuss sexuality with their daughters, a sympathetic and knowledgeable person (e.g., nurse or counselor) should be available to answer her questions. A refusal to divulge information about human sexuality when that information is sought by the victim will only heighten her fears. Honest responses to her questions will help her to gain control, reduce her confusion, and trust you.

- If the victim is an adolescent, the rape may compound communication problems which already exist. Do not force her to self-disclose, but if she expresses a desire to talk about the assault, be prepared to do so. She can benefit from talking about the experience, if it is *her* decision to talk. Also, attempts to help your child "forget" about the rape by refusing to discuss it may give her the impression that you are ashamed of her or hold her responsible. It is also important that a professional trained in child sexual victimization be available to provide guidance.

- If your daughter was raped by a date or other person she knows, she may fear that you will hold her responsible for using poor judgment. She may fear that she will be punished, that she will not be believed, or that you will take matters into your own hands and cause her to be ostracized by her peers. In anticipation of your responses, she may conceal information from you (e.g., the use of alcohol), or otherwise act out in ways which further undermine her credibility in your eyes. Again, it is important for you not to judge or punish her for what happened. She needs to know that you believe her, that you do not second-guess her judgment, and that there will be no unnecessary restrictions on her activities. Equally important, do not display more concern for what others might think (i.e., family reputation) than for your daughter's recovery needs. Knowing that she does not have to fear your reactions will be a positive step in her recovery.

- Encourage your daughter to resume her normal lifestyle, such as playing sports and seeing friends. Limiting your daughter's emerging independence by "grounding" her for not being sufficiently careful, will seem like punishment to her and could cause resentment. It is important that her rights concerning dating, seeing friends, involvement in extracurricular events at school, as well as her responsibilities for household chores, remain the same. Being overly protective of her can make her recovery more difficult.

- If your daughter is very young, she may show signs of distress through a change in behavior, rather than by articulating what is bothering her. Behavioral reactions in young children are common and should be monitored closely for frequency and severity. Be alert for the following signs:

» loss of appetite

» withdrawal

» altered sleeping patterns or nightmares

» fear of being touched

» fear of undressing

» fear of other people

» bed wetting

» wanting to hide

» excessive outbursts of crying

» violent or destructive acts

» self-mutilation (e.g., intentionally cutting one's self)

» preoccupation with sexual themes in the course of playing or conversation

- As we have mentioned, it is common for rape victims of any age to have flashbacks. For a young victim, however, such flashbacks can cause her to seem almost "frozen" in a horrible moment and thus not be very responsive to the immediate environment. These terrible mental images during a flashback seem to take control of the victim and compound her mental and emotional turmoil. As a parent, you may be able to help your daughter regain her grounding in the present by adjusting her attention through sight, hearing, or touch. Listening to tranquil music, seeing comforting photographs, or touching something safe and familiar, such as a stuffed animal, can diminish the flashback and help her

to regain her composure. The important
thing is to direct her senses to that which is
safe and familiar so that she regains some
control.

- Young victims of sexual assault are likely to
have concerns about their sexual identity.
This is true regardless of whether the victim
is a heterosexual, a lesbian, or otherwise unsure about her sexual orientation. Such concerns, complicated by the rape, are not
something that your daughter will likely
want to share with you. Honor her need to
discuss these concerns with sympathetic and
knowledgeable persons who can respond ap-
propriately. Under no circumstances should
you use her victimization as an example of
why she should change her sexual behavior.

- If the crime is reported to the authorities
and the victim is a child, parental permission
may be required for medical treatment and
for police questioning. Be available to provide such authorizations and any additional
information needed by medical and police
personnel.

- Because fear of the unknown usually is
worse than fear of the known, carefully explain why your daughter needs to cooperate
with medical and police personnel. Avoid
springing any surprises on her.

- The gynecological exam may also be a first-
time experience and can be extremely upsetting unless parents and medical staff are
sensitive. Gently convince your daughter
that the procedure is necessary, but insist

that the medical staff carry out the exam with patience and sensitivity. If it is appropriate and your daughter desires the support, allow a trusted person to be present during the medical exam.

Additional Parental Concerns

- If your daughter is an adolescent, monitor her for the consumption of drugs and alcohol. Among those already prone to experiment with drugs or alcohol, there may be a sharp increase in use following a sexual assault. Such "self-medication" should be strongly discouraged. If you learn that your daughter is using drugs or alcohol, consult with professionals who know who know how to deal with both the substance abuse and the rape victimization.

- Do not let your daughter use her victimization to manipulate you inappropriately. Fathers sometimes have a difficult balancing act between being supportive and being pushed to do things that are contrary to their best judgment. Although your daughter's routine activities will be disrupted for a time following the assault, her responsibilities for school, household tasks, or extracurricular activities should not become points of negotiation. She needs to know that, even as you love her and support her recovery, you are consistent in your role as a parent.

- A decline in your daughter's school performance may occur after the rape. As a parent, you must strike a balance between making sure that she performs well as a student, while you help her to work through the emotional complications associated with recovery. If there are academic difficulties, it is appropriate to consult with the school counselor. In this case, the need to respect confidentiality must be tempered with the need to ensure your daughter's academic success. Sharing information with school professionals on a "need to know" basis is a reasonable course of action. Teachers and school counselors are in a position to modify academic tasks and provide support in ways that can aid her recovery. If you do consult with school personnel, however, you should tell your daughter and explain the reasons why.

In giving support to your daughter, we recognize the difficulty of controlling your intense feelings in order to place her recovery needs first. Again, blaming the victim or making threats of revenge against the rapist are counterproductive and should be avoided. We want to emphasize again that you should not hold yourself responsible for the rape or for failing to protect her. It is virtually impossible to create an environment in which the possibility of rape is completely eliminated.

There are no magic formulas for you to make everything right for your daughter. The most important message is simple: *you love her no matter what.* The dividend for your unconditional love is the realization that you are providing a solid foundation for her successful recovery.

6
Understanding Acquaintance Rape

The majority of rapes (approximately four out of five) involve perpetrators and victims who are known to one another. The term "acquaintance rape" often is used to describe a sexual assault committed by someone the victim knows, including casual acquaintances, classmates, teachers, employers, family members, and "friends." The term "date rape" applies to a subset of acquaintance rape and refers to coerced or unwanted sexual activity within the context of a dating relationship, including first dates and current or former partners. Because the traditional one-on-one date may no longer be the social norm for many young people, the term "date rape" also can apply to unwanted sexual encounters that emerge out of group activities such as parties and dances.

For our purposes, it is useful to distinguish between acquaintance rape and stranger rape because the responses of victims and others may vary, depending upon whether the perpetrator is part of the victim's social circle. Criminal law, however, does not make such a distinction. A victim's lack of consent is the critical concern, regardless of whether the perpetrator is someone she knows.

Of all age groups, young women of high school and college age experience the highest rates of sexual assault by persons they know. Young females, however, are much less likely to report sexual assault by acquaintances than by strangers. These victims often suffer in silence without legal redress or the support of counselors, family, or friends. There are many reasons why a victim of acquaintance rape does not reveal the assault to the police or to others who could be supportive. Among such reasons are the following.

- She had voluntarily consumed alcohol or other illicit drugs prior to the assault. Her memory of events, her belief that perhaps she placed herself at risk, and her desire not to divulge her use of alcohol or drugs affect her decision to remain silent.

- She had been sexually intimate with the perpetrator in the past (e.g., a former boyfriend) and she doubts that her claim of rape will be believed by others, including the police. Because she once cared about this person, she may also wish to avoid "getting him into trouble."

- She had engaged in a degree of consensual intimacy (e.g., kissing or petting) and now believes that she is responsible for "allowing" what happened to occur. She may also believe that she failed to communicate her

sexual intentions clearly enough, thus "causing" him to "go too far."

- She is deeply embarrassed by what happened and does not want others to question
her conduct, judgment, reputation, or her
decision to associate with certain people.

- She does not define the event as rape, even
though she did not consent to what happened.

Acquaintance Rape Sequence

Many men have a difficult time comprehending
how a woman can be raped by someone she knows.
It is helpful to think of acquaintance rape as a
gradually unfolding process rather than as a sudden
attack. Consider the situation of many female high
school and college students whose active social lives
regularly involve them in parties, informal gather-
ings, school activities, and other settings where they
are in contact with young men. Understandably,
most females assume that such settings are a desirable way to meet new friends and potential partners.
Male perpetrators—persons who often seem attractive and well liked by females—use these circumstances to select possible targets. In these myriad
social encounters, where young females come to
know someone at least casually, it is normal and understandable for them to presume a certain degree of
trust and want to be on good terms. Unfortunately
for many victims of acquaintance rape, their trust
and desire to be friendly are used against them by
self-serving and egocentric "nice guys" . . . guys who
seize the opportunity to sexually exploit their vic-

tims under circumstances where there is a low probability of getting caught.

Although no two acquaintance rape scenarios are necessarily alike, there are common elements. A social gathering where alcohol flows freely is a typical setting for perpetrators to begin the process of target selection. Perpetrators use peer pressure to encourage high rates of alcohol consumption among females, particularly those who may have little experience with functioning under the influence. Simply stated, "feeding drinks" to possible targets is one of the most common strategies employed by perpetrators in the beginning of the sequence.

These males also use flattery and give their potential victims "undivided attention" in a gradual process of desensitization. They often view relationships with females as a game of conquest where deception is acceptable. The ideal victim is someone who is under the influence of alcohol or drugs, is flattered by the attention, and who appears to be controllable. The perpetrator typically attempts to separate the target from others by suggesting that they go to a room or other private location. He also engages in subtle forms of physical and psychological intrusion. This may include gradually escalating touches, sexual themes in conversation, and the exchange of other "personal" information. In effect, the victim is being "groomed" for a "sexual encounter" (the perpetrator never defines it as rape). In other words, the victim's actions can be made to seem to others—and possibly to her—as if she "wanted" this to happen.

If the encounter progresses to kissing and caressing, the perpetrator typically escalates in more physically intimate ways (e.g., touching her genital area; attempted removal of clothing) in order to see if she responds in a reciprocal, consenting manner. Often the victim puts up with his advances even as she subtly tries to dissuade him. Her wish to spare his feelings and her belief that she can control his actions work to her disadvantage. Her "no" is interpreted by him as a "maybe" or a "yes," and he persists despite her responses. Alone with him, with one or both persons possibly under the influence of alcohol, and with her having "allowed" a certain degree of consensual intimacy such as kissing to occur, the perpetrator becomes progressively more aggressive in his sexual advances. He ignores her words and actions that communicate her lack of desire for a sexual encounter. Through his conduct, he implies that she will not be able to leave until she submits to his advances. Often she feels pinned down and unable to resist or escape, even if he does not use overt physical violence or threaten her with a weapon. Despite her lack of consent, he may say things such as "It's okay" or "You are great" as he violates her.

His actions throughout are meant to suggest that this is a consensual sexual encounter, even though she gave no consent. Afterward, he may talk to her in a way that suggests he simply complied with her wishes. Often he will indicate that he will contact her for another "date," thus implying that a "relationship" between them exists. His goal is to confuse her and make her feel responsible. He also wants her to remain silent about what transpired. If she divulges what happened, invariably, he will distort her actions to make it seem that she invited a consensual sexual encounter. After all, who can claim otherwise?

Put simply, at the heart of the perpetrator's actions is a deliberate strategy of desensitization, intrusion, deception, manipulation, intimidation, and denial. His conduct is an abuse of power that is not created by the victim's actions. Lacking her clear consent, his behavior constitutes a sexual assault and should not be thought of as a "seduction" or simply a "miscommunication."

Her confusion after such an event should not be seen as complicity by her. In part, her confusion and that of others following such a scenario reflects widely held beliefs in our culture that after a certain degree of intimacy such as kissing and caressing, males have sexual rights over a woman regardless of her objections. The burden seems to be placed unfairly on the female to recognize at what point he can no longer control his "natural urges," thus implying that she is responsible for his unwanted aggressiveness.

Consequences for Victims

The effects of acquaintance rape on victims can parallel those involving stranger rape, but may also differ in certain respects. As we have suggested, stranger rape is more likely to be reported to the police than acquaintance rape. In addition, victims generally receive more support from family and friends if they are assaulted by a stranger. In cases of acquaintance rape, there is often a lingering suspicion that she "should have refused his advances" more clearly and forcefully, and that her actions triggered "uncontrollable desires" in the perpetrator. In other words, acquaintance rape involves a high degree of victim blaming.

To the extent that the rapist has friends within the same social circle as the victim, her potential support system is undermined and her version of events will be called into question. Her own feelings of responsibility are intensified by mutual friends who claim that "he's not that kind of guy." Often she is silenced out of fear that she will not be believed or that others will claim that she provoked him.

If she was violated by someone she trusted, there are other consequences as well. The victim may now believe that she is a poor judge of character, thus experiencing self-doubt and apprehension when meeting new people. Unfortunately, this apprehension may gradually develop into a generalized distrust of all males, including those who are worthy of her trust.

If the perpetrator is a family member, the effects on her and on others are devastating as family bonds are destroyed. Family members often take sides, as if rape were a simple dispute and not a criminal act. Victims often feel that they are responsible for tearing the family apart and for causing a scandal.

If the victim decides to take legal action against an assailant whom she knows, the difficulties she experiences can be compounded by police responses. Police are generally reluctant to pursue rape cases where the "alleged" victim and perpetrator are known to one another and possibly involved in a "relationship." Where physical evidence and witnesses may be difficult to obtain, and where the victim may have been under the influence of alcohol and may have agreed to some degree of physical intimacy with the assailant, the police tend not to treat this as a criminal case. The police and prosecuting attorney may simple ignore rape cases where the victim's account is difficult to corroborate or prove in court. Acquaintance rape, especially if it involves a current or former dating partner, is most likely to be dismissed by law enforcers as "unfounded" and, therefore, not worth the time and trouble to investigate. The reasons for unfounding charges of rape against acquaintances include the following.

- There is a tendency to view the reported episode as a "lover's quarrel" rather than a serious sexual assault.

- There is a belief that the alleged victim will drop all charges after she has had time to "cool down."

- If caressing and sexual foreplay occurred prior to the assault, there may be a belief that she "assumed the risk" and gave tacit consent to intercourse. A belief that she was being promiscuous or intentionally seductive (a "tease") often undermines her credibility.

- Law enforcers may believe that if the victim had a prior sexual relationship with the man, she could be lying or exaggerating in order to seek revenge.

- There may be a lack of physical evidence (e.g., bruises; abrasions; torn clothing), medical reports, or eyewitness accounts to substantiate the charge, thus rendering the complaint "her word against his." Delays in reporting make obtaining physical evidence especially problematic.

- There are witnesses who know both parties whose accounts might cast doubt on her version of events.

- The victim had voluntarily consumed illicit drugs or was inebriated at the time of the assault, thus affecting her credibility and the accuracy of her memory.

- The police believe that she is greatly exaggerating her claim (or lying) because by claiming victim status, she is getting attention.

It is clear that police response—or lack of response—to her claim that she was raped can compound her recovery by adding to her anxiety, self-doubts, and frustration. If police dismiss the case, others may take this as evidence that she was not victimized. She now has to contend not only with what the rapist did, but also with the system response to the attack. Simply stated, the tendency to dismiss her claim of rape, or the suggestion that she is exaggerating or being untruthful, harms her recovery.

How You Can Help

There are several ways you can be supportive if she has been sexually assaulted by an acquaintance. The following suggestions will help.

- Again, reassure her that you believe her story, regardless of the actions of police or others who know of the incident.

- To counter any self-doubts about her ability to judge character, convince her of a simple truth: it is impossible to know in advance who will be a rapist. Neighbors, friends, former partners, fellow employees, classmates and new acquaintances may only need the right opportunity for rape to occur. Rape is not about her judge of character or her actions; it is about the abusive behavior of the rapist.

- Remind her that even if she was initially friendly to the rapist, she absolutely is not responsible for causing him to "lose control." Demonstrations of affection and friendship by her do not make her liable for his abusive actions.

- It is important to help diffuse a generalized feeling of distrust that she may have developed. Such distrust can function to isolate her and further complicate her interactions with others. She needs to feel that her assailant is not representative of all males, and that trust is essential for developing healthy, intimate relationships. Indeed, your relationship with her should model the value of openness and trust.

- If the assailant was a family member, your first concern should be with the needs of the victim, regardless of the consequences for the perpetrator. Neither her recovery nor simple justice can be served if the rapist is shielded by family members from the consequences of his actions. In addition, in the absence of an effective response, there is a heightened risk that the assailant will repeat the behavior.

- If she voluntarily consumed drugs or alcohol, do not let that be the focus of your discussions because it will seem that you are blaming her. If you are concerned about substance abuse, seek guidance from a counselor on how best to address this as a separate issue, rather than as the reason why rape occurred.

- Adolescent victims of acquaintance rape are especially concerned about becoming the object of gossip and ridicule among their peers. Although it is impossible to control such insensitive behavior, it is appropriate for you to discuss what words and actions she might employ that will help her to respond effectively to unfortunate remarks by others.

- Finally, regardless of whether she presses charges, encourage her to get medical attention and to contact a rape crisis center.

Understanding Your Reactions

If the rapist is a friend or family member, you probably will feel a profound betrayal of trust that parallels the victim's feelings. You may also question your own ability to judge character. It is likely that you have other friends who operate in the same social circle as the rapist. This can be very awkward for you, for the victim, and for those persons who wish to avoid taking sides. Furthermore, rumors about the rapist's version of events, and general gossip about the reputation of both the rapist and the victim, may continually confront you and her. This is especially likely if both the victim and the assailant are in the same school or work together.

As we have indicated, it is inappropriate and dangerous for you to seek revenge against the rapist, even if he can be located without difficulty. It is best to have no communication with this person, even if there should be chance encounters in hallways or other locations.

In addition, if mutual acquaintances remain on good terms with the assailant, you may feel betrayed by them. Their actions could also fuel doubts in your mind about what happened and about the credibility of the rapist's story. It is a sure bet that the rapist will deny culpability. The most common defense in acquaintance rape cases is a distorted claim that the victim consented to have sex, or that no sexual activity took place. You may be tempted to think, "After all, if the people we know still think this guy is okay, maybe it didn't happen the way she said." Such lingering doubts are especially common if you are the sexual partner of the victim. Again, do not think of the rapist as a sexual rival. Given such thoughts, it is also a challenge for you to avoid blaming the victim, but that is the very hurdle you must overcome. To quell such doubts, ask yourself a simple question: Who has the biggest motivation to lie? The answer, of course, is the rapist.

Regardless of gossip or the responses of others, your loving relationship with her should be the basis for understanding what has transpired and what to do to help her recover. In short, do not let others inadvertently jeopardize the trust and understanding that is the basis of your relationship with her. In light of these complexities surrounding acquaintance rape, it would be helpful for you to keep in mind the following summary of points.

- No woman wants to be forced into sexual relations. The rapist, even if he is someone you know, is not in competition with you for the affections of the person you love.

- You cannot control what others think or say, nor should you try. Your belief in her and you continued support are what matter.

- Do not feel guilty if an element of doubt crosses your mind. Such thoughts are not unusual but almost certainly are based on false assumptions or distorted accounts by others.

- Neither you nor the victim is responsible for what happens to the assailant if charges are filed with the police. It is the responsibility of the courts to decide his fate, regardless of any pressure that the family or friends of the rapist may bring to bear upon the victim or you.

- Do not isolate yourself from friends who know of the rape. Neither of you have reason to feel shame or guilt. Remember, your true friends will be understanding and supportive.

Clearly, the consequences of acquaintance rape pose special challenges for you and for the victim. The bottom line, however, is the same. You can hasten her recovery by letting her know that you believe her, that you will stand by her throughout, and by being consistent in your love.

7

Special Cases: Interracial, Gang, and Drug-Facilitated Rape

Some instances of rape require special consideration because they pose unique challenges for victims as they struggle to recover. Interracial rape, gang rape, and drug-facilitated rape are three such special cases.

Although the majority of rapes occur between persons of the same race, estimates suggest that approximately 10 percent of reported rapes involve victims and perpetrators who are not of the same race. Reported interracial rapes most often involve African American assailants and Caucasian victims. The key word, however, is *reported*. There is evidence that African American and Hispanic women are less likely to report interracial rape than is true of Caucasian women. Distrust of police and concern over possible negative responses among members of their community may contribute to the lower reporting rates among women of color.

Interracial rape tends to evoke especially strong feelings of outrage among those close to the victim, particularly males. Racial prejudices and tensions, coupled with the sexual and emotional complexities associated with any rape, create a volatile mix. Constantly expressing strong feelings about racial issues in the aftermath of the rape, however, may further confuse and traumatize the victim. It is also true that the victim's own responses to interracial rape may be organized around racial themes. To the extent that racial hostility becomes the focus of interactions, her recovery may be impeded. As a key support person, your task is to help deal with the reactions of the victim and those close to her that may inappropriately focus on race as the central concern.

The complications involved in this form of sexual assault are not limited to race. The same recovery concerns can be associated with various ethnic or religious groups, or even persons of different social classes. To the extent that prejudicial feelings already exist toward persons of that group, such feelings are themes that need to be addressed in her recovery.

In most instances of interracial rape, the perpetrator is a stranger. Perhaps this is because casual social contact typical of acquaintance rape occurs less frequently when males and females are of different racial or ethnic groups. Interracial rapes tend to occur in settings where the victim is accessible and vulnerable, such as parks and parking lots, where she may be attacked without warning. Often a weapon is used to force her to submit. Many of these attacks occur in broad daylight as the woman performs her daily routines. Consider the following scenario.

Jane, an African American female, is in the midst of her daily jog through the city. As she enters a residential area which adjoins her own neighborhood, she is suddenly knocked to the ground by a white assailant. A knife is placed to her throat and she is forced into a nearby alley and raped. Throughout, the rapist uses derogatory sexist and racist slurs. Jane is brutalized and terrified. Afterward, when she manages to return home, she immediately tells her husband of the assault. What kinds of reactions might there be to the rape? The following are illustrative.

- Jane and her husband might conclude that the rape was a racially motivated hate crime. Such a conclusion is especially likely in areas where considerable racial tensions already exist, and when the perpetrator makes references to the victim's race.

- Since Jane is black and her assailant is white, she may be reluctant to report the rape to the police. Many racial minorities lack confidence in a legal system which they feel may not fairly represent their interests. Jane may also be reluctant to seek the help of others, including professionals, who are not perceived to be sensitive to the issues raised by persons of color.

- In cases of interracial rape, anger toward the rapist may generalize to all members of his race. Rather than coming to grips with her feelings toward the rapist, the victim may "resolve" the incident by concluding that *all* white males (or black males if the victim is white and the assailant is African American) are enemies. Simply stated, she may experience fear and distrust of all members of that race and suffer from panic attacks in their presence. Because daily routines often involve interracial contact, such reactions can be a serious impediment to her recovery and to her ability to carry out normal routines.

- Relationships with friends and acquaintances who are of the same race as the assailant may be affected adversely. Some women find themselves avoiding these acquaintances and therefore lose a portion of their support system when it is most needed. It is also true that friends who are of the same race as the perpetrator could prove instrumental in dispelling the victim's tendency to generalize negative attributes by race or culture. These friends could serve as powerful role models of compassion and trust.

Negative reactions involving a generalized anger toward all members of the assailant's race are also experienced by males close to the victim. The key point to understand is that focusing on the rapist's race distracts the victim from addressing a basic concern—*her feelings about that particular person.* To help her in ways that will promote her recovery, the following are important guidelines.

- You, family, and friends must avoid making racial slurs. Such comments may inappropriately encourage her to develop generalized fear and distrust along racial lines.

- Remind her that not all males of the perpetrator's race are potential rapists, racists, or
  untrustworthy. If she has close friends of
  that race, point out that these individuals
  have been and will continue to be deserving
  of her trust and friendship. If you notice her
  avoiding contact with these friends, you can
  suggest that she discuss this with a counselor.

- Reassure her that you do not hold her responsible for the assault, and that in no way
  do you consider her to be "unclean" because
  she was raped by a person of another race.

- Since interracial rape so often occurs while
  the victim is in the midst of her daily activities, encourage her to resume those activities
  as soon as she is able. A refusal to venture
  out could signal that racial fears are hinder-
  ing her recovery.

Remember that even if the rape appears to include a racial motive, the rapist's motive is not the
central issue in her victimization. The violence, injury, and degradation that one human being imposes
upon another is the real tragedy of rape and this
should be the focus of your efforts to help her.

Gang Rape

Although there are examples of high profile media coverage of gang rapes, this form of sexual violence generally has not received much attention,
perhaps because most rapes involve a single perpetrator. As such, comparatively little is known about
various forms of gang rape. What is known is that

gang rapes, when compared to single offender assaults, are more likely to involve extreme physical
brutality (including torture) and verbal degradation.
These rapes also extend for a longer period of time—
sometimes hours—where the victim suffers multiple
assaults. Victims of gang rape see their offenders as
more violent, they feel even more terrified, they feel
less able to fight back or escape, and are more likely
to have a protracted period of recovery when compared to victims of single offender assaults.

Because gang rapes tend to be so violent, it is
essential that the victim receive immediate medical
attention. Certainly there is an elevated risk of sexually transmitted infections that must be monitored.
It is also essential that she have professional counseling available. The trauma of gang rape is such
that victims often experience extremely low self-esteem, depression, and a higher risk of suicide. They
often report that they "feel like garbage."

There are several contexts in which gang rape
finds expression. One of the most common examples
of gang rape occurs during war. Invading soldiers,
with few restraints on their conduct, use gang rape
as an instrument of terror and torture. Such rapes
may even be encouraged "unofficially" by those in
command. In a sense, rape is one of the "privileges"
of the victors, or a spoil of war. Sadly, victims of
gang rape in the context of war seldom receive treatment or any means of legal redress.

In peacetime, however, gang rape takes a different form. It is most commonly associated with all-
male groups such as sports teams, fraternities, and
youth gangs. Male bonding in these groups is such
that there is peer pressure to demonstrate one's

power and "sexual prowess" in public ways. Fraternities or team members, for example, may hold parties where an opportunity arises to take advantage
of one or more victims who are drunk, drugged, or
otherwise unable to extricate themselves from a
situation where they are overwhelmed. Typically
these perpetrators will explain their conduct as
"group sex" with a willing partner, not rape. Such
activity may be part of a rite of passage for new
members to demonstrate their loyalty to the group.
Often they will brag openly about what happened,
calling into question the honor and reputation of the
victim.

Similar dynamics operate with youth gangs.
Many male gangs have a contingent of females who
serve as quasi members and who are involved in
various degrees with gang activities. Females who
wish to join the gang are often required to go
through an initiation. In the language of the gang,
they are "sexed in." This means that they are coerced into "having sex" with any number of gang
members. In effect, these initiation rites are gang
rapes.

There are at least three underlying dynamics in
these gang rapes. First, such rapes are public expressions of misogyny . . . the hatred of women. For
these perpetrators, women are merely objects to be
used, humiliated, and to serve male interests. Second, these gang rapes function to create a powerful
bond among the assailants—a bond which enhances
each member's sense of superiority through domination of others. Such group action becomes the stuff
of legend among the members . . . at the expense of
their victims. Finally, gang rape serves the purpose

of openly demonstrating one's heterosexuality through "sexual conquest." To partake in such a public event is a way to show male friends that you are "manly" and not gay. By helping the victim to understand these dynamics, you will also be helping her come to terms with a question that haunts her: "Why did they do this to me?"

Another concern that may haunt her is what this will mean for her reputation. Very often the offenders are acquaintances of the victim who operate in the same social circle (e.g., school). She is likely to fear that others will think she is a "slut." It is certain that the perpetrators will claim she consented to have "group sex." In other words, they will collectively shift responsibility away from themselves to the victim by claiming "she wanted it." The physical and emotional damage they have inflicted upon her is now made worse by the harm they are doing to her reputation. Gang rapes are, in effect, public events that are the basis of gossip and speculation about the victim's character and responsibility.

Furthermore, because gang rapes often occur in the context of parties, the police may also believe it was consensual "group sex." No doubt stereotypes of wild student parties enhance the mistaken belief that "orgies" are common.

Not only are gang rape victims likely to be blamed for their victimization, but they are also likely to encounter their assailants daily on school grounds or other locations. Such encounters are disquieting reminders of the rape. There may also be peer pressure and subtle threats made against her to keep her quiet.

For these reasons, we again stress that you tell her you believe her, that you know her actions did not trigger this event, and that her reputation is not tarnished. She needs to know that you will support any legal action she decides to take against the assailants, and that you will help her withstand attempts by the offenders and their friends to intimidate her into dropping charges. It is also important that you do not press her to initiate a lawsuit against an organization (e.g., a fraternity or school) if it is contrary to the victim's wishes. Such legal action has a high probability of publicizing the event and causing people she knows to choose sides. Because she may want to avoid this, no legal action should be taken unless she gives her consent.

Drug-Facilitated Rape

In recent years, we have seen the emergence of a new and troublesome problem known as drug-facilitated sexual assault. Of course, alcohol is a drug that is long associated with rape. Drug-facilitated sexual assault does not refer to consumption of alcohol or street drugs such as cocaine or marijuana, but to a class of drugs that have sedative properties that can affect muscle control, perception, and memory function. Two drugs in particular have been used widely in drug-facilitated rapes—GHB and Rohypnol. Both are powerful central nervous system depressants with effects that include sedation, loss of inhibitions, and memory impairment. These effects are intensified if either drug is mixed with alcohol. The result is a high level of "intoxication" that is experienced rapidly; usually within 15 minutes of ingesting these drugs.

There are two general ways in which these drugs can come into play in rape cases. One way is for the drug to be given intentionally to the victim without her knowledge. Often it is slipped into a drink in liquid or powder form where it is difficult to detect. The other way is for the victim to voluntarily consume the drug and as a result, a sexual predator takes advantage of her vulnerable state.

When a person unknowingly consumes a drug, it is referred to as involuntary intoxication. The law treats involuntary intoxication as special in two ways. First, the person who unknowingly consumes the drug is not seen as responsible for the consequences of her actions while under the influence. This can include her ability to give meaningful consent to sexual acts. Second, the law severely punishes any person who is responsible for involuntarily intoxicating another. For example, the U.S. Congress passed the Drug-Induced Rape Prevention and Punishment Act in 1996. This law can result in a twenty year prison sentence for a person who gives a controlled substance to another person without their knowledge, with the intention of committing a sexual assault.

The difficulty in addressing involuntary intoxication is that the victim may not be sure if she was drugged, or be able to clearly recall if she was raped. (Waking up eight hours later in a strange location, with a spotty memory, and experiencing vaginal or rectal soreness, are indications of what may have happened.) In addition, timely testing for drugs in a toxicology lab is problematic. Apart from the availability and costs of drug screening, Rohypnol and GHB do not stay in one's system long. Samples of the first urine after consumption of these drugs is important, but few drug-facilitated rape victims are in a position to save such a sample.

In cases where the woman voluntarily consumed the drug, such action does not make her responsible for being raped. Sexual predators look for opportunities to take advantage of a female who appears to be extremely intoxicated. The law generally treats as special cases those rape victims who are passed out or who otherwise are in no position to give meaningful consent to sexual acts because they are intoxicated (even if they chose to become intoxicated). In such cases, the responsibility can and should be on the perpetrator to demonstrate the manner in which he claims he obtained consent for sexual acts. Simply stated, her lack of ability to give consent is the legal concern, not her decision to use drugs.

To summarize, there are several ways you can help her to come to terms with drug-facilitated rape. We recommend the following.

- She should know that it is a federal crime if someone gave her a controlled substance without her knowledge. Help her to weigh all available legal options.

- Remind her and others that her behavior while under the influence of a drug did not invite rape. Reassure her that she is not responsible for what happened while she was drugged.

- Calm her anxiety if she is not able to recall the details of what happened. Because memory impairment is common with certain drugs, her lack of recall does not mean that she is trying to hide something.

- If she voluntarily consumed illicit drugs and was raped, do not let her drug use be the focus of concern. It will only complicate your relationship with her if she believes that your primary interest is with her decision to use drugs, rather than her being raped.

In each of the special cases discussed, there is a common thread . . . the need for your sustained patience, love, and acceptance. Trust that with your support, she will overcome the challenges posed by any of these circumstances surrounding her rape.

8
Reporting the Rape

An important decision each rape victim must make is whether to report the crime to the police. Unfortunately, rape remains one of the least reported crimes. Evidence consistently suggests that perhaps no more than 25 percent of rapes (possibly less than 10 percent) come to the attention of the police. Among the reasons given by victims for not reporting rape to the police are the following.

- having had a prior intimate relationship with the assailant (e.g., an "ex-boyfriend")
- in cases of acquaintance rape (especially involving close "friends" or former partners), uncertainty whether the assailant's conduct constitutes rape
- a belief that she somehow "allowed" this to happen
- shame, embarrassment, guilt, fear of being blamed, concern over her reputation
- fear of reprisal

- concern about how this will affect her loved ones if the rape is disclosed
- belief that there is nothing the police can or will do
- stress associated with becoming involved in complicated legal proceedings
- fear that the legal system will do one more harm than good
- distrust of the police, especially if one has experienced callous behavior from officers
- fear that one's own conduct (e.g., alcohol or drug use, sexual history) will become the focus of police investigation or made public
- desire to protect the rapist, especially if he is a family member or "friend"

Perhaps out of a desire to punish the rapist or out of fear that he will rape others, many victims are willing to report the rape and testify in court. This is a courageous decision, given that a rape trial is anxiety-producing and emotionally exhausting for victims. It is important that the decision whether or not to press charges be made *by the victim.* You should support her decision, whatever it may be. In order to provide maximum support for her if she decides to pursue legal options, it is important that you and she understand the procedures initiated when the rape is reported (summarized at the end of this chapter).

The collection of evidence begins with a preliminary police interview (perhaps at the crime scene) and a medical examination. The medical exam should be conducted by a trained Sexual Assault Nurse Examiner (SANE) or physician who will record and treat her injuries. If she is in critical need of care, no preliminary interview should take place until she has received medical treatment. The sooner the police are notified and she is examined, the greater the likelihood of obtaining solid evidence. Reporting to the police, however, merely gives the victim the option of later prosecution. Even if she reports the rape, it does not automatically mean that the case will go to trial.

As indicated in a previous chapter, the medical exam ideally is conducted before she can bathe, change clothing, eat, or use the restroom. This means that some of the evidence which can be *felt* on her body, including the perpetrator's semen or other bodily fluids, needs to remain intact. Her body, in a sense, is a crime scene. A pelvic exam, STD tests, combing and pulling of pubic hair, oral and rectal swabs, fingernail scrapings and other procedures are common.

As you can imagine, such an exam, carried out by strangers in the immediate aftermath of a rape, can be extremely unsettling. One way you can help is by requesting that a Sexual Assault Response Team (including a SANE professional) be in charge of this process. Such a team includes a victim advocate who is trained to help her through the trauma of police questioning and medical examination. Also, ask for a private waiting area for her so that she does not have to sit in an emergency room awaiting the exam. Finally, you can help by being available to answer questions that may arise.

Shortly after the medical exam, a detective will be assigned to the case and arrangements made for the victim to give a formal statement. Police questioning at this point is usually lengthy and emotionally draining. Remember, she is in the impact phase of the assault where she may be experiencing disorientation, fear, and a range of emotional extremes. The questions themselves could throw her into a state of pre-impact terror or trigger unsettling flashbacks. Because of this, she may not remember accurately all of the details, or she may choose not to answer all the questions completely in an effort at emotional self-preservation.

Questions asked during this impact phase, in effect, bring the victim to a place where she does not want to go. She may even recant her story to avoid further interrogation. Clearly, this is a critical time for her and for law enforcement. She may be less than forthcoming as a self-preservation measure at the very time the police require accurate information. Her behavior does not mean that she is being uncooperative or is lying. If the recounting of the incident seems "contradictory," there are probably good psychological reasons why this is happening. Unfortunately, she may not realize the importance of every word she says to the police. Problems in the statement she gives to the detective could come back to haunt her at the trial where the defense attorney will attack her credibility. That is why it is important law enforcement to review her comments at a later time, when she is progressing in her recovery, to ensure the accuracy of the information.

The other complication is that anything the victim says to police may not be held in confidence. She will be asked about her prior sexual involvements (including her last consensual sexual act), her alcohol and drug use, her associations, her conduct just prior to the assault, and specific details of the sexual conduct of the rapist. You can imagine her reluctance to discuss such information with a stranger, knowing there is no guarantee that this information will remain confidential. If you are her husband, father, or boyfriend, you can understand why she may also be reluctant for you to learn of such details.

Rape victims do not always contact the police immediately after the assault. Days or weeks may pass as she attempts to sort things out on her own. Because you are loved and trusted by her, you may be the first person to whom she speaks about the rape. In this case, your immediate concern is to make sure that she receives medical attention as soon as possible.

Being the first person to hear of her victimization has another implication. If she reports the crime to the police, be prepared to provide them with your own statement. She may have told you details that she failed to recall when questioned by the police. Police consider "excited utterances," often disclosed by victims to the first person they talk to about the crime, to be important evidence. Under such circumstances, the victim may feel an added responsibility for "dragging you into this situation." Convey to her that your concern is for her well-being, and that assisting the police is not an inconvenience for you, especially if it means bringing the assailant to justice.

Given the deeply sensitive nature of rape evidence, you want to help her throughout the process of evidence collection. This may mean finding a balance between shielding her from additional trauma, and not interfering with police questioning. The fol-

lowing are things you can do to be helpful at this difficult time.

- Remind the police to coordinate with victim
  service professionals to reduce the number
  of times she has to recount the rape. Re-
  peated telling of the event (to detectives, the
  district attorney, counselors, family and
  friends) is emotionally exhausting. If allowed
  by police and if she agrees, encourage that a
  victim advocate be present during police
  questioning.

- She may request that you be present when
  she discusses the incident with detectives.
  Being with her at this moment can provide
  reassurance and make her feel less alone. It
  is very important, however, that you do not
  interrupt or interfere with police questioning. Despite your good intentions, it is not
  helpful for you to answer questions for her.

- She may request that you *not* be present
  during police questioning. A reluctance to
  disclose details of the rape in your presence
  does not mean she is rejecting you or disre-
  garding you feelings. If anything, she may be
  trying to protect you from being overwhelmed. Remember, it should be her decision to discuss the rape with you on her
  terms, at a time when she feel it is appropriate, perhaps without strangers being present. Respect her wishes and do not feel that
  she is slighting you.

- Many women feel more comfortable if a female officer is conducting the interview (especially in cases of acquaintance rape). If

such a person is available, remind the victim
to request her for the duration of the questioning.

- Most victims do not know what to expect
  when being questioned by police. She may be
  upset and confused if many people are involved in securing information and asking
  questions that require her to repeat what
  she has already said. Standard police procedures may seem bureaucratic and insensitive
  from a victim's perspective. Whenever possible, remind the police to explain to her why
  they are proceeding in a particular fashion.
  Asking questions about procedure is not an
  implied criticism, but a way to reduce confusion and a sense of powerlessness.

- If the victim uses sign language or does not
  speak English, do not ask children or other
  family members to translate the victim's account to police. Inform the police of her need
  for an interpreter so that they may provide
  one.

- Because of the lengthy nature of most police
  interviews, she may have gone without food
  for a long period. If she is hungry, offer to
  provide her with a hot meal.

Following her interview, the police will attempt
to locate and question the suspect if he has been
identified. There may be sufficient evidence for an
immediate arrest. The district attorney's office will
be notified to discuss prosecution options. Law enforcers may decide against prosecution if they believe that the evidence is weak or circumstantial.
Simply stated, the complaint of rape may be desig-

nated as "unfounded." A classification of "un-founded" may mean that law enforcers believe her but do not think that the case will result in success-ful prosecution. The label "unfounded" should not be confused with a false report. A false report sug-gests that the police know that the alleged victim did not tell the truth. An "unfounded" classification could mean that they are unsure of her account, but usually means that either there is insufficient evi-dence, or that evidence was collected improperly and would not likely be admissible in court. Among the reasons for "unfounding" a claim of rape may be the following.

- delay in reporting by the victim (weeks, months, or years have passed since the rape)
- previous victim-assailant intimate relation-ship (former lovers)
- evidence that the victim was intoxicated or using illicit drugs at the time of the assault
- refusal to undergo a medical exam
- failure to preserve relevant physical evi-dence (e.g., torn or stained clothing; semen)
- perception that the victim "assumed the risk" (e.g., hitchhiking; getting drunk and going to his room; agreeing to "heavy pet-ting" or other forms of intimacy and then "changing her mind")
- she alters her story after filing a police re-port
- circumstances associated with the incident are atypical and do not fit a "standard pat-tern" commonly found by investigators

- victim is hostile toward law enforcers and is perceived to be uncooperative
- because of a disparity in where the victim lives and where the crime took place, charges may have been filed in the wrong jurisdiction

In addition to these reasons, a victim may be discouraged from filing charges if she is perceived to lack credibility as a witness. For example, seldom is a prostitute successful in bringing forth a charge of rape; law enforcers will not think she will be believed. A victim's lifestyle and appearance can be factors that may result in law enforcers discouraging a victim from bringing charges. One example is an elderly or extremely obese victim of rape. There are those who will think, "Who would ever believe that someone would want to rape her?". Law enforcers often have a mental profile of whom they consider to be an ideal or a poor witness. Unfortunately, factors such as the victim's appearance, relationship to assailant, consumption of alcohol or drugs, and lifestyle may serve as subtle influences on how claims of rape are treated.

If the police and district attorney agree that a crime has been committed, but that it is not a "good" rape case, they may decide to prosecute the assailant on charges other than rape (or sexual battery). Possession of stolen goods, simple assault, breaking and entering, or a range of other sexual assault charges (e.g., attempted rape; gross sexual imposition; importuning; public indecency) may be used. If authorities charge the perpetrator with offenses that seem of lesser significance than the rape, the victim may feel that she is not believed or that the crime of rape is not being taken seriously. Let her know you understand that rape, first and foremost, is the primary concern in her recovery, regardless of the charges that may be brought against the perpetrator.

Filing charges sets in motion a lengthy and emotionally exhausting legal process wherein the truth of the victim's story may repeatedly be called into question. Once charges have been filed, the crime is viewed as an action against the state, with the woman serving as a chief witness on behalf of the state. The judicial system, from her perspective, seems to depersonalize what is to her a singularly terrifying personal experience. Medical and other personal information become part of the court record.

Information about the crime may appear in the paper because court records are available to the media. Some persons in the media, however, are sensitive to the victim's request to keep rape cases out of the public spotlight. If it is her wish, you could run interference on her behalf with the local media to keep her name and other information from being mentioned.

Shortly after charges are filed, depending upon the laws in her particular jurisdiction, the victim may be asked to testify before a grand jury (or only the judge). The function of a grand jury is to determine if there is sufficient evidence to indict the accused. To this point, she has recounted the rape to individuals, but now she has to speak in front of a *group* of strangers. Some victims find this to be especially difficult. If the victim fails to appear in court for this preliminary hearing, charges against the assailant may be dropped. (If the criminal case does not proceed, she still has the option of filing a lawsuit against the perpetrator to seek compensation for damages.)

Once the victim completes this process, she may be called upon to provide additional information in preparation for a trial. If agreed upon by the district attorney, she may request to see the police reports on her case to check their accuracy. In addition, she has every right to be protected from unwanted contacts by the defense attorney or family and friends of the perpetrator. Let her know that she is not required to speak to the defense attorney, even though that person may approach the victim as if she has no legal choice. Any such unwanted contacts should be documented and the district attorney notified. Finally, remind her to ask about victim compensation or restitution options. Many jurisdictions have funds available to crime victims to cover medical and other costs incurred as a result of the crime.

Throughout this process, your patience and support is essential. Again, you can help by reassuring her that her decision to pursue legal action is not only the right thing, but is also an act of courage.

Reporting a Rape: Typical Procedures

The Immediate Aftermath
- Reporting of incident to the police
- Initial police interview
- Medical examination
- Identification of weapons or other evidence gathered by the police

The Investigation

- Identification of the assailant (examining mug shots or developing composite sketch if a stranger)
- Interview with a detective
- Apprehension of suspect if he is known
- Charges filed with the district attorney

The Criminal Justice Process

- Testimony before a grand jury or judge
- Probable cause found (sufficient evidence to merit an indictment)
- District court arraignment where the assailant pleads guilty or not guilty
- If plead guilty, sentencing date set; if plead not guilty, trial date set

9
Going to Trial

Once the assailant has been indicted, there is typically a three-to-nine-month waiting period before the trial begins. This is a particularly difficult time for the woman for several reasons. First, her assailant may post bond and hence remain free to "walk the streets." She is likely to experience an understandable fear that he will seek revenge, although restraining orders should help protect her from this possibility. Also, family and friends of the rapist may call her and attempt to persuade her to drop the charges. Likewise, the defense attorney may attempt a number of delay tactics in the hope that she will not pursue the case. Perhaps most important of all, the woman is placed in a position of having to keep the incident in the forefront of her consciousness, remembering all of the details, until after the trial. In other words, during the pre-trial period she is given little opportunity to put the incident behind her and get on with her life.

The Pre-trial Period

This pre-trial period requires great patience, understanding and support on your part. She may exhibit a number of physiological and emotional patterns which you find distressing (e.g., nightmares, insomnia, loss of appetite, fatigue, depression, tension headaches, and generalized anxiety). It is at this point that your relationship with her may undergo the greatest stress. It is not uncommon for some men to feel annoyed at her for being "too emotional" and insist that she cease talking and thinking about it. Some men develop a sense of resentment toward the woman for having to spend increased time with her or because she seems unresponsive to the man's needs. Patience can only add to the quality of your relationship in the long run. We urge you to keep in mind two things.

1. She did not choose this situation and feelings of anger and resentment will only add to her distress.

2. The difficult period she is going through is temporary and is likely to diminish once the trial has ended.

A common experience among victims waiting for the rape trial to begin is a considerable degree of apprehension about serving as a witness. Such anxiety is normal and understandable when one considers the fact that many victims have never even seen the inside of a courtroom, much less having to speak into a microphone in front of a group of strangers. Her anxiety may be compounded if there is poor communication from the police and district attorney's office concerning the dynamics of the legal process and what is expected of her as a witness.

Furthermore, like most people, she may have only a vague idea of standard courtroom procedures, the meaning of legal and medical jargon relevant to the case, or proper courtroom decorum when testifying. Little wonder if she has serious doubts about wanting to endure a trial.

To make matters worse, victims frequently come to feel that they are pawns in a legal chess game where they have no power to decide things which affect them directly. There are seemingly endless delays in finally bringing the case to trial. Typically the defense attorney will *deliberately* seek court delays as a tactic to discourage the victim. This is especially difficult for witnesses who must rearrange work schedules or travel from a long distance to testify. You should do all you can to encourage the district attorney to demand a speedy trial. The victim should have a right to protection against frivolous requests for delays. Likewise, the district attorney should be discouraged from making decisions about her case without consulting her. Unfortunately, most of her contact with the police and district attorney's office will be at their convenience, not hers. In a very real sense, the impersonal character of the legal system can function to dehumanize the rape victim and further strain her emotional resources.

In order to help her regain a sense of control and prepare her for what to expect in court, there are a number of things you can do. Although no two cases are exactly alike, the following suggestions are of use in helping her prepare for trial.

- Encourage her to request from the district attorney a copy of her signed statement given to the police shortly after the incident.

This statement is important evidence and re-
viewing it will refresh her memory of the
event. If there are discrepancies between
this statement and subsequent courtroom
testimony, the defense attorney may claim
she is an unreliable witness in an attempt to
discredit her. It is very important that she
remember the detailed sequence of events to
avoid appearing confused on the witness
stand. Preparing for trial is like preparing
for an exam; studying her earlier statement
is an important way to avoid inconsistencies
in the testimony.

• Another way to help her recall significant
details is by accompanying her to the scene
of the crime, *if she agrees*. Because of the po-
tentially disturbing nature of such a visit,
she alone should make this decision. However, visiting the physical location will help
her describe it in court and may stimulate
her recollection in other important ways. In
addition, a visit to the crime scene may occur
in the process of the trial anyway; if so, a
prior visit with you will help.

• To familiarize her with the setting, accom-
pany her to the courtroom several days in
advance of the trial. Pay special attention to
the position of the witness stand and the di-
rection she will face when giving testimony.
If possible, it may be that you, a counselor,
or a trusted family member could sit in public seating located directly in her line of vi-
sion from the witness stand. If she has a
sympathetic face to look upon while testify-

ing, rather than the defense attorney or assailant, it may help to ease her tension.

• Because she has to describe in detail what transpired during the rape, she needs to be comfortable with appropriate terminology to describe sex acts. This will help her avoid the use of "slang" terms which may discredit her.

• Double check with friends or other witnesses who have been subpoenaed to testify at the trial. Make sure they are aware of the correct time and location of the trial, and if necessary, help them arrange transportation or baby sitting.

• If the defense attorney asks to talk to her, she is under no legal obligation to do so and may refuse. Likewise, if she or those close to her receive threatening communications from the family or friends of the rapist, the district attorney should be informed. She is entitled to have the district attorney protect her from such harassment.

• Make sure she is mentally prepared for the possibility of last minute delays or for a plea bargain before the case goes to trial. If it is clear that the victim is determined to stick with the case despite various delay tactics, many assailants will plead guilty to a lesser charge (e.g., attempted rape) in order to avoid the possibility of a longer sentence. Although the decision to accept a plea of guilty to reduced charges is made by the district attorney, at least it has the benefit of sparing her the ordeal of a trial. Also, a plea bargain cannot be appealed later on. You may request that any decisions made by the district attorney should involve prior consultation with her.

- Finally, request that the prosecutor's office be committed to having a single prosecutor manage the case from the filing through the completion of court proceedings. There are several reasons why a rape victim's case should not be shuffled around to several prosecutors. Having a single prosecutor from start to finish means that the victim does not have to repeat her story each time a new person is brought on the case. A consistent account of what happened, and trust between the victim and the prosecutor, together increase the likelihood of a successful prosecution. In addition, a single prosecutor has another advantage. Defense attorneys may see a change in prosecutors as an opportunity to negotiate a more advantageous plea bargain. Simply stated, an earlier plea offer by a prior prosecutor often can be parlayed into "a better deal" with a new prosecutor who is less familiar with the case. Also, a change in prosecutors often means delays in concluding the case. Such delays tend to discourage victims and witnesses and generally work to the advantage of the defense.

Many women find the rape trial to be a negative experience, though for some it is therapeutic. Usually the most difficult aspect of the trial is the fact that the woman is called upon to publicly testify. This means that she must reveal the details of her rape to a group of strangers and be subject to cross examination by an attorney who will attempt to attack her character and question her version of events. Frequently the defense attorney will ask leading questions that imply a history of sexual promiscuity. Some victims feel that it is they who are on trial, not the assailant. Many states now have laws (often referred to as "rape shield laws") that limit questioning about the victim's sexual history. However, information about past sexual relations between the victim and the accused is admissible.

Finally, the trial itself is another time the victim must confront her assailant face to face. In a very real sense, she is alone in front of a crowd, speaking publicly of a deeply private and humiliating experience. Without the support and understanding of you and others close to her, the courtroom experience threatens to further traumatize her and undermine her feeling of self-reliance.

Giving Testimony

During the trial, the defense attorney is likely to defend the rapist using one of three arguments.

1. The rape never took place and the story was invented by the woman in order to seek revenge or simply call attention to herself.

2. The rape did take place but the defendant was mistakenly identified as the assailant.

3. The woman was not a victim of rape but a willing participant in sexual intercourse.

Regardless of the approach taken by the defense, the victim usually has her character and judgment called into question during the cross- examination. The defense attorney may claim that she was too hysterical to make positive identification; that she fabricated events to "get even" or because she wants others to think she is sexually attractive; that she is sexually promiscuous and would have intercourse with anyone; that her "misconduct" (e.g., drinking) precipitated the event; or any other argument that undermines her credibility as a witness. Remember that the role of the defense attorney is to create doubt in the minds of judge and jury, so both she and you should be prepared to encounter accusations about her character and stereotypes about how women should act in various situations.

In order to prepare her to present testimony (or prepare you if you are a witness), there are several points to keep in mind.

- If possible, answer all questions directly without appearing uncertain. Statements such as "I don't know" or "I'm not sure" tend to raise doubts among the judge and jury.

- Be prepared for interruptions while giving testimony. People may wander in and out of court or the attorney may request a recess even though the testimony is in progress.

- While testifying, it is helpful to speak in a clear and deliberate manner. Take your time before responding to questions and maintain eye contact with the jury and others in the room rather than staring at the floor.

- Being properly dressed and well-groomed enhances the credibility of the witness. Do not wear blue jeans, shorts, T-shirt or tennis shoes to the courtroom. Do not chew gum; the judge or jury might find it distracting.

After the Trial

Despite the difficulties of a rape trial, hopefully there is an important consolation—the conviction of the victim's assailant. At the very least, the trial provides the victim with an opportunity to express her anger toward the rapist and feel a degree of justice being served. During and after the trial, it is important to convey to her that she is not "changed" in your eyes and in no way should she feel guilty for what happened in the courtroom. Because cross-examination tends to promote feelings of self-doubt, inadequacy, and confusion, it is especially important that you reassure her of your continued faith in her judgment and character. Many victims emerge from a rape trial with anger and resentment toward a legal system that seems to "protect the criminal and condemn the victim." A heightened sensitivity on your part to the difficulties of a rape trial is a great asset in maintaining a positive relationship.

Given the nature of rape cases, there is a distinct possibility that the offender will go free. If this occurs, under no circumstances should you or others close to the victim attempt to take justice into your own hands. Rather, there is one other legal avenue that the victim can pursue. She has the right to sue the rapist for damages. Such action would be a *civil* case rather than a criminal one, and she would have to assume legal expenses.

In a civil action, the burden of proof ("preponderance of evidence") is somewhat less stringent than is required in a criminal trial ("beyond a reasonable doubt"), and it is necessary only to establish that the victim suffered harm as a result of the defendant's action. Also, a unanimous jury verdict is not required for the victim to win a judgment, and it is possible also to sue third parties (e.g., fraternities, businesses) who should have anticipated and attempted to prevent the rape.

Of course, a successful civil action will not put the rapist in jail, and the victim is responsible for retaining a lawyer and absorbing legal fees. Nevertheless, such actions may help deter rape, and the monetary award can help compensate for lost wages.

If the rape involved a college student and took place on campus, the victim has the option of filing a complaint with the campus judicial officer, regardless of whether there is a criminal charge. Virtually all colleges have judicial processes that deal with charges of rape involving students. The goal of these campus hearings is to determine if a student's conduct violates school policy. If a student is determined to have violated the school's sexual assault policy, he may be dismissed immediately.

Once legal action has been completed, it is helpful to discuss with her the likelihood of future contacts with the rapist. Working together to determine ways of coping with or avoiding such encounters may help reduce anxiety. For example, you have the right to request notification of when a convicted rapist will be released from prison. In addition, you must both be aware that the successful completion of legal action will not "make everything right." For one thing, if the rapist appeals the conviction, it may result in a second trial which again requires her to be a witness.

Much of the fear, anger and hurt could continue to persist after the trial. She may even feel responsible for the fact that a man was sent to prison, even though he was found guilty. Simply remind her that the judge and jury determined his fate, not she. Moreover, many rapists have committed *multiple* offenses and her courageousness in going to trial may save other women from a similar ordeal.

Victim Assistance Programs

In recent years, many states have passed legislation mandating a variety of benefits and services to assist victims of violent crime. Because these programs vary considerably from one state to another, only a very general summary can be given here. Your local police department and rape crisis center can provide you with details on the services available in your state.

The benefits and services may include:

- Financial compensation provided by the state and monetary restitution from the offender.

- Victim/witness assistance services, which include programs designed to keep the victim apprised of possible plea bargaining negotiations, pretrial release, and scheduling of sentencing and parole hearings. Also, some states allow for the introduction of "victim impact statements" at pre-sentence hearings. These statements detail medical, financial, and psychological damage caused by the crime, including changes in the victim's family relationships.

- Finally, most states have passed a "victim's bill of rights," which may require, among other things, that victims be made aware of the programs and services described above, notified of all court proceedings, provided with child care and other social services (if needed), and protected against intimidation by the accused or his family and friends.

The effectiveness of these programs and services has not been systematically evaluated. However, the fact that they exist is evidence of increased sensitivity to the plight of violent crime victims. It is also noteworthy that police training in most areas now pays special attention to the needs of rape victims. Although seeking legal action against a rapist may be a difficult ordeal, the overall climate regarding the treatment of rape cases appears to be improving for victims.

10
Protecting Against Rape

Once a woman has been raped, it is common for her to experience prolonged and deep-seated fears concerning her safety. Unless one has had the experience of being the victim of criminal assault, it is difficult to understand why others who have been victims appear to be preoccupied with personal safety. Given the violence of rape, it is understandable for victims to feel an enduring sense of uneasiness or tension about everyday events that others take for granted. Fear of strangers, fear of going out of the house, fear of dating, and fear of being alone are just a few examples. It is important for you to realize that fears concerning personal safety, although seemingly "silly" or "unreasonable" from an outsider's standpoint, are rational and understandable from the victim's point of view. Furthermore, her state of mind is not likely to change simply because family or friends tell her that her fears are "ridiculous."

For both stranger and acquaintance rape situations, overt physical resistance to an attack may help or may further endanger the victim. Some claim that proficiency in self-defense techniques can provide an additional measure of safety. There is evidence that this is true. Others suggest that passive resistance and persuasion may dissuade an assailant. The simple fact is that no one can say what is *always* the best response to an attack. Characteristics of the assailant and the circumstances will vary. All one can say with certainty is that anything which helps the victim to survive an attack is the right thing to do.

Reducing the Risk of Stranger Rape

Although it is true that there is no foolproof means to prevent future assaults, there are some steps to be taken which may ease a rape victim's fears and enhance her safety. The following are suggestions you and she can consider.

- Make sure her home is safe with dead-bolt locks on doors, peep-hole viewer and window locks. Change the locks when moving to a new residence.

- If a stranger should come to the door, do not allow him in or indicate that no one else is home. Ask delivery or service persons for identification and do not allow children to ask strangers into the house. Make phone calls for strangers when there is an emergency. If a woman is alone in the house, she should pretend there is someone else home when a stranger visits.

- Women living alone may choose not to list the first name on mail boxes or in telephone directories. In apartment complexes, avoid remaining alone in laundry rooms, basements, or garages. Make sure the entrance to the house is well-lighted.

- Always keep car doors locked, including when driving, and park in lighted areas. Before getting into a car, check the back seat. If there is car trouble, open the hood, attach a white cloth to the door and remain inside the locked car. If followed in a car by a stranger, drive directly to the police station.

- If one cannot avoid being alone on the street or a college campus late at night, stay in areas which are lighted and carry a police whistle. Try to avoid walking in places with dense woods or shrubs which could hide an assailant. Never hitchhike!

Reducing the Risk of Acquaintance Rape

For parents, efforts to prevent acquaintance rape among daughters require some understanding of the complexities of adolescent dating. Many parents have a difficult time discussing dating with their daughters, and may resort instead to restrictions on her behavior to protect her from rape. Such actions are *not* recommended, as they do not help her develop the skills she needs to assess and avoid problem situations. Moreover, such actions are likely to produce conflict and poor communication.

In discussing the possibility of acquaintance rape with your daughter, focus on ways of developing and maintaining healthy dating relationships. The following are helpful points.

- It is perfectly acceptable to refuse a date and not feel guilty for doing so. It is a mistake to go out with someone out of guilt or because of peer pressure.

- Males who constantly act "macho" should be avoided. Observing such displays in possible dating partners can be a signal of potential future problems.

- Do not be afraid to communicate limits concerning the desired degree of physical contact. No one has the right to force or manipulate another into undesired sexual acts, and it is important to learn to say no. Do not hesitate to let another know when touch makes you feel afraid, confused, guilty or manipulated. It is your right to set limits when physical contact makes you feel uncomfortable.

- Relationships that evolve gradually may be safer and more stable than "whirlwind romances." It is desirable to get to know another better before becoming emotionally and physically committed. A successful relationship is more likely if it develops gradually out of a sincere friendship.

- Relationships change. Assure your daughter that she has the right to end a relationship that is no longer healthy or fulfilling.

- Perhaps most important of all, remind her that healthy dating relationships are based on equality. The most successful relationships are those where partners share equally in the privileges and responsibilities of the relationship.

It is our experience that few parents discuss with their daughters whether they might be entering into a relationship with a male who is possible violent or exploitative. To avoid such unhealthy relationships, alert your daughter to males who exhibit the following behaviors.

- He has violent outbursts where he hits or throws objects at you, particularly when he is under the influence of alcohol.

- He has been violent toward former partners.

- He always has to "win" an argument or fails to respect your needs and views when there is a disagreement.

- He views your accomplishments as threatening.

- He discourages you from having other friendships or tries to isolate you from others who care about you.

- He boasts of sexual intimacy as a victory or achievement.

- He forces or manipulates you into engaging in sexual activities when it is against your wishes.

- He has threatened suicide (or violence toward you or others) in order to keep you in the relationship.

- He views you as his property, subject to his control, and become upset when you do things without his "permission."

As a parent, it can be difficult to stand back and let your daughter take risks. The reality, however, is that a certain degree of risk taking is part of growing up. You might consider making a "safety contract" with your daughter. If she calls you and asks to be picked up, no matter what time of day or night, you agree to do so . . . no questions asked at that time.

There is one additional concern that you should discuss with your daughter. The Internet provides sexual predators with many opportunities to make contact with potential victims. These sexual predators are not always adults, but often are other teenagers. For example, many adolescents who use chat rooms to discuss with peers favorite music, films, or hobbies, find that they receive an unwanted online sexual solicitation. It is important for you to know of your daughter's use of the Internet and to discuss with her any such solicitations.

There is one additional concern that you should discuss with your daughter. The Internet provides sexual predators with many opportunities to make contact with potential victims. These sexual predators are not always adults, but often are other teenagers. For example, many adolescents who use chat rooms to discuss with peers favorite music, films, or hobbies, find that they receive an unwanted online sexual solicitation. It is important for you to know of your daughter's use of the Internet and to discuss with her any such solicitations.

Because acquaintance rape so often emerges in the context of relationships with classmates, it is worth your while to find out what kinds of sexual assault awareness programming is offered at your daughter's school. We believe that sexual violence is a public health concern that should be addressed in school curricula. If such information is offered at her school, this poses a perfect opportunity to discuss with her the health and safety issues that most concern you.

11
Finding Help

Throughout this book, we have emphasized what husbands, fathers and male friends should and should not do in order to help rape victims recover. Because such a heavy demand is placed on men to be supportive, they too need assistance. Helping men is critical to helping victims.

In each community, there are likely to be several possible sources of help. Community mental health centers, pastoral counseling services, and private practitioners are but a few possibilities. There are also a number of national organizations dedicated to helping victims and their families.

In addition, over the past decade, hundreds of rape-crisis centers have been established in communities throughout the United States and Canada. These centers specialize in addressing the needs of victims. Many also provide services to family members and friends of victims. Some centers run groups for men and offer them short-term counseling. Virtually all will make referrals to help men locate services not available at the center.

Despite the value of the services offered, our research indicates that relatively few husbands, fathers, and male friends of rape victims seek assistance at these centers. Many males mistakenly believe that rape crisis centers are places only for women. Unfortunately, this misconception is reinforced by those who refer to these places as "women's centers." A more appropriate term would be "recovery centers" because in most instances, services are available to both men and women as they strive to deal with the aftermath of sexual assault.

Another reason why males may not seek help at rape crisis centers is based on their beliefs about the staff who run these centers. It is true that the majority of staff members at rape crisis centers are female. Because the issue of rape has been identified with the feminist movement, some males are likely to believe that they would be unwelcome intruders at rape crisis centers. They may believe that they would encounter hostility, or at the very least, the female staff would not be understanding or sympathetic to their concerns. In reality, many males who use rape crisis center services find a positive reception and a willingness by staff to provide them with help.

Finally, many males are reluctant to seek help because they believe that needing assistance is a sign of weakness. They find it difficult to be open about their emotional vulnerabilities. Males need to understand that getting help is not a symptom of weakness or an admission that they "can't take it." Rather, it is a realization that there are those whose professional training places them in a position to offer useful advice at a time of great need. Seeking help is a way to gain strength and to preserve a relationship with a loved one.

12
A Final Note

We wish to stress once again that *you* are in a strategic position to help a loved one recover from rape. But her recovery will take time and there are no miracle cures. By realizing that through sympathetic understanding you will exert a positive but necessarily limited influence, you can avoid the tendency to take personal responsibility for her ultimate happiness. By being patient, supportive, and non-judgmental toward her you will be communicating the most important message---your unconditional love. Finally, trust that she is strong enough to do the rest on her own.

Appendix A
Illustrative Case
Studies*

While there are many possible reactions to the rape of a loved one, the following case studies will help you to understand proper and improper responses. These case studies illustrate many of the things one should and should not do when dealing with a rape victim. The most important point to remember is that the husbands, fathers and male friends of rape victims can be helpful or they can be harmful. With patience and understanding, men can minimize the terror and degradation experienced by women who have been raped.

Case Study 1
Wendy: A Teenage Victim

The Incident

Wendy, a fourteen year old girl, was spending a few days with her girlfriend Betsy and Betsy's family at their summer cottage. One afternoon Wendy and Mark, Betsy's 16-year-old brother, paddled the canoe

---

*Despite alterations, the names and situations in these illustrative case studies are substantively accurate and represent real experiences.

to the far end of the lake—a heavily wooded area where there were no other cottages. Mark told Wendy that he had a bottle of wine and asked her if she would like to sit on the bank and drink with him. Always a rather adventuresome child, Wendy agreed to Mark's suggestion.

Although Mark drank the lion's share of wine, Wendy had a sufficient amount to feel light-headed and rather silly. Perhaps mistaking her elevated spirits as an indication of flirtatiousness, Mark put his arm around Wendy and began to kiss her on the lips. This was the first time Wendy had ever been kissed and, being rather taken back, she literally did not know how to respond. What's more, Mark did not stop at that point but aggressively began petting her. This frightened Wendy, but her inexperience in these matters caused her to be passive and not say anything. Suddenly Mark removed his bathing suit and told Wendy to do likewise. Frightened and confused, Wendy said she wanted to go back to the cottage. With a forceful tone, Mark said everything would be "all right" and that there was nothing for her to fear. In a rapid series of moves, he pulled off the bottom of Wendy's suit, pushed her on her back and entered her. In a state of shock, fear, confusion, and physical pain, Wendy could only cry.

Although the entire episode lasted a few minutes, Wendy continued to cry for a long time. Her emotional state began to frighten Mark. Through her tears, Wendy managed to say "Why did you do that? You shouldn't have done that to me!" Mark clearly was scared. He tried to console her by indicating that it was only normal for people who liked each other to "make love." Then he said, "Besides, you should have said something earlier if you really didn't want to."

After returning to the cottage Wendy said nothing to Betsy or to the parents. In fact, Wendy said nothing to her own parents after she returned home. However, her emotional state and her behavior were definitely altered. Wendy was not clear as to her responsibility in the matter. She was certain that her parents would be angry with her if they knew she had been drinking. Even though her parents noticed that Wendy appeared to be moody and uncommunicative, they assumed it was merely a "phase."

Shortly after the new school year began, Wendy became ill at school for several consecutive days. Upon recommendation from the school nurse, Wendy received a medical exam which revealed that she was pregnant. Neither she nor her parents had suspected her condition.

Others React

The revelation of Wendy's pregnancy produced extreme anger in her parents, particularly her father. He could barely contain himself as he screamed his demands that she explain herself. Because Wendy had never communicated about sexual matters with her parents, she found it extremely difficult to discuss the event, especially with her father. Her understandable reluctance only served to escalate his anger to a point where he threatened to kick her out of the house. Finally, she broke down in fits of weeping and managed to describe what had happened.

Wendy gave an honest account to her parents, though her inexperience in the area of sexuality deeply embarrassed her and compounded her difficulties in communicating. Wendy had many unanswered questions in her own mind, but the anger of her parents made it difficult for her to share those questions and receive feedback. She had questions about her own sexuality, about the nature of pregnancy, about whether others blamed her, and about what would happen to her friendship with Betsy and other peers. In addition, Wendy had great concern over what should be done with the baby and whether or not she would be able to finish school. The anger and shame of her parents only added to the depression Wendy was feeling.

Without asking Wendy's opinion, her parents decided to send her away to a special school for the duration of her pregnancy. When the child was born, it would be placed for adoption without Wendy ever seeing it. In addition, her father sought legal action against Mark and his parents on a wide variety of charges. Again, this action was taken without consulting Wendy. Furthermore, Wendy was denied the right to see her group of friends. Her every move was carefully scrutinized by her father. Finally, Wendy's entire family engaged in a "conspiracy of silence" wherein her "encounter" (they avoided using the word rape) and subsequent condition were never mentioned by anyone.

Although Wendy's parents meant well, her feelings about what was happening seemed to be of secondary importance to the feelings and wishes of her mother and father. It was clear that her parents, especially her father—whose will usually prevailed in family matters—were embarrassed by the situation. They tended to blame Wendy for poor judgment.

Even though Wendy received proper medical attention, her parents never sought to provide her with counseling. In a state of utter depression, feeling isolated, insecure and guilty, Wendy attempted to take her life. Although she survived the attempt, her physical and mental state were such that she had to be hospitalized for a lengthy period of time.

In the spring, Wendy gave birth to a baby girl whom she never saw. Although that was several years ago, the impact of those events is still very much evident in her life. Wendy has continued to receive professional help but her emotional recovery has been slow and very painful.

Lessons to be Learned

In a sense, Wendy became a multiple victim of a single crime. She was victimized not only by rape, but also by an unwanted pregnancy and a lack of understanding in the home. Unfortunately, her situation is similar to that of many teenagers who have been raped.

In almost every instance, the reactions of her parents, especially her father, compounded Wendy's emotional trauma. Rather than communicating unconditional love and support, Wendy's parents communicated anger and embarrassment.

When Wendy's parents learned of her rape and pregnancy, a calm and understanding approach was in order. The anger and threats of her parents made it difficult for Wendy to express her feelings. She was being blamed for poor judgment and lack of character when in fact, her only "fault" was a lack of understanding and experience in sexual matters. Unfortunately, Wendy was never provided with an appropriate resource person with whom she could have frank discussions about sexuality and pregnancy. In the absence of information, Wendy's fears continued to grow.

At every phase in the decision making process, Wendy should have been given the opportunity to share her feelings. Decisions affecting her should not have been made without her input. This is especially true in respect to the decisions made for her about her schooling and her baby.

Wendy's parents also made the mistake of isolating her from her network of friends at a time when she most needed them. Limiting contact with her peers (including her friend Betsy) reflected her parents' shame rather than an awareness of Wendy's needs. Concern over the family reputation seemed to be more important than addressing Wendy's emotional needs. Finally, the "conspiracy of silence" prevailing in the home communicated to Wendy that her behavior was too terrible even to be discussed. Feeling guilty, confused, isolated and unable to communicate with those persons she loved most, it is not surprising that Wendy's depression led to an attempted suicide.

What Wendy's Parents Should Have Done

- **Wendy's parents should have responded to her need for unconditional love.** Parents who spend time blaming others or themselves for the rape of their child waste valuable time and energy. This energy should be directed toward reassuring and supporting the victim.

- **Wendy's parents should have let her know that someone would be willing to talk to her about adult intimacy.** Since the rape was Wendy's first sexual experience, Wendy needed reassurance that her fears and questions about adult intimacy could be discussed. Such a discussion with either her parents, a trusted adult, or a counselor, would have helped Wendy realize that her capacity for sexual intimacy in adulthood had not been diminished.

- **Wendy's parents should have arranged for professional assistance to help the family communicate more effectively.** Unfortunately, counseling to help Wendy deal with the rape, her pregnancy, and her parents' reactions was not provided until after Wendy's attempted suicide. Early professional assistance would have improved the communication between Wendy and her parents. Communication between parents and adolescents is often strained even under normal conditions. During the crisis produced by rape, effective communication is made even more difficult. Improved communication, paired with greater understanding and support at home, would have spared Wendy and her family a great deal of unnecessary pain.

- **Wendy's parents should have allowed Wendy to return to her normal activities.** By encouraging Wendy to resume her normal lifestyle as much as possible, her parents would have provided her with a much

needed sense of normalcy. It also would
have increased Wendy's access to her friends
and peers who could have provided important support.

- **Wendy's parents should have been
  more considerate of her rights and
  feelings.** Such consideration would have
  helped Wendy to not feel punished and ex-
  cluded. When Wendy's parents refused to
  discuss with her the rape experience and her
  future, they communicated that they were
  ashamed of her and that they held her responsible for being assaulted. Had Wendy's
  parents listened to her and included her in
  the decision making process, she would not
  have felt so isolated and could have taken an
  active role in her recovery process.

Case Study 2
Carla: A Case of Acquaintance Rape

The Incident

Carla is 28 years old, single, and teaches ele-
mentary school in a suburban community. While returning to her apartment from a dance class one
evening, she was approached in the parking lot by
her former boyfriend, Ron. Although they had
stopped dating—by mutual agreement—nearly a
year ago, Ron still called her from time to time.
Carla sensed that he had never totally accepted the
fact that their relationship was over. On this occa-
sion Ron seemed distraught. Even though she could

smell alcohol on his breath, Carla agreed to let him come inside and talk about what was troubling him.

Once they were inside her apartment, there was an abrupt change in Ron's mood. He became very belligerent and aggressive. He told Carla that even though she was now dating another man, she would always be his girl. Carla could tell by now that Ron had been drinking heavily. She became concerned for her safety. She recalled two occasions during their dating relationship when Ron was physically abusive to her after he had been drinking. She tried to calm him down and offered to make coffee, but Ron was too drunk and angry to listen to reason. He told her that he thought it would be the "right thing" for them to make love. Carla strongly refused. He then slapped her and forced her into the bedroom where he raped her. Afterwards, he warned her not to say anything to anyone and joked that even if she did, no one would believe her anyway.

As soon as he left, Carla composed herself somewhat and tried to decide what to do. Should she report the rape to the police? If she did report it, would the police believe her? After nearly an hour of soul-searching, she decided to call her boyfriend, Dale. She was confident that Dale would believe her and would help her decide on the right course of action.

Others React

Dale arrived within 15 minutes and Carla, though considerably upset, told him what had happened. Dale was shocked and confused by her story. He wanted to ask her what she was doing with Ron in the first place and why he was in her apartment. However, he realized that Carla needed support and advice, not questions. Although Dale said it was her decision, he advised her to report the assault to the police. Even though the police might question a charge of rape against a former boyfriend, Dale felt that Carla would have to bring charges against Ron or run the risk of being raped again. Carla agreed. Within two days, Ron was arrested and charged with rape. Shortly thereafter, he was indicted at a preliminary hearing and a trial date was set.

Meanwhile, Carla returned to work after a week's leave of absence. She and Dale tried to resume their normal pattern of social activities. Privately, though, Dale was having doubts. Carla had told him several times that her relationship with Ron was over. However, she had said also that Ron called her occasionally to "talk about old times." In addition, a mutual friend of Ron and Carla's told Dale that she had known Ron for several years and found it difficult to believe he would force himself on Carla. Ron, for his part, was strongly denying that he had raped Carla, even though he admitted to having sexual relations with her that night. After all, he reasoned, they had virtually lived together at one time and had continued to maintain regular contact with one another.

Dale felt guilty for doubting Carla's version of events, but the doubts would not go away. At the same time, they stopped socializing with many of their friends because a number of them were also friends of Ron. Several mutual friends had hinted that Carla probably agreed to have sexual relations with Ron, later calling it rape to preserve her relationship with Dale. As the strain on their relationship grew, Carla and Dale argued more frequently and were no longer able to communicate openly with each other. Finally, Dale confronted her with his suspicions that she had fabricated the rape charge to cover up her own promiscuity. Carla wanted to prove to Dale that his suspicions were unfounded. However, his unwillingness to trust and support her convinced her that it was not worth the effort. She thus became increasingly isolated from Dale and her friends.

To make matters worse, the district attorney decided that there was not sufficient evidence to yield a conviction. As a result, the case was dropped. In Dale's mind, this confirmed his worst suspicions about Carla's fidelity and honesty. No longer able to effectively communicate, Dale and Carla ended their relationship. Since then Carla has lost contact with a number of her former friends and has found it increasingly difficult to resume dating other men.

Lessons to be Learned

The impact of Carla's rape on her relationship with her male friend, Dale, is similar to that of many other cases of acquaintance rape. Initially, Dale appeared supportive and understanding. He did not pressure Carla with questions but rather attempted to do what was best for her. However, Dale's ability to be supportive gradually eroded in the face of his doubts about her honesty and fidelity. In attending to the comments of their mutual friends, Dale allowed casual gossip to cloud his trust of Carla. He therefore jeopardized their ability to communicate. Dale could have been more helpful to Carla and himself if he had approached the situation differently.

What Dale Should Have Done

- **Dale should have applauded Carla's willingness to help a friend in distress (even if that friend was a former lover).** Instead of communicating doubts about her honesty, he should have demonstrated his trust in Carla and his love for her by not letting his anger dominate their relationship. Had Dale realized the trust Carla had placed in him by confiding in him, he may not have doubted her fidelity.

- **Dale should not have been influenced by gossip.** Allowing the gossip of associates to influence his decision only worked to the disadvantage of preserving his relationship with Carla. It would have been much better if Dale had stood by Carla to help her fend off rumors, rather than abandoning her at the time of her greatest need.

- **Dale should have considered professional counseling.** A professional counselor could have helped Dale realize that the expression of friendship which Carla extended to Ron did not imply any desire for sexual intimacy. Through counseling, Dale would have learned to reassure Carla that she was in no way responsible for Ron's sexual assault upon her.

Case Study 3
Lisa: Rape Victim with Nonsupportive Partner

The Incident

At approximately 3:00 a.m. on a hot summer night, Lisa was awakened from a sound sleep by the presence of someone in her bedroom. At first she thought it was her four year old son Tommy, but an instant later she was frozen in terror when the figure of a man hovered over her and said, "Bitch, I'm gonna rape you; if you scream, I'll go after your kid." Lisa's terror was so complete that she could neither speak nor move. She was engulfed in a sensation of "unreality," almost as if she were watching a movie rather than being the victim of a horrifying event. As the man began to remove her bed clothing, Lisa's immediate concern was for the safety of her son and so she did not fight her assailant.

As the stranger descended upon her, Lisa managed to say, "Please! Please don't!" In a half mocking, half vengeful voice the man replied, "I've been watching you and I think you're gonna like this." Reeking of alcohol and whispering profanities in her ear, the man proceeded to rape her. The room was dark and Lisa never saw his face. After 10 minutes, which seemed like an eternity, the stranger started to leave. He turned back to Lisa, "If you try calling the police, I'll be back. This is between you and me— if I have to come back, you and your kid won't be so lucky next time." With those words, the rapist bolted through an open window into the night. Lisa ran into Tommy's room, saw that he was undisturbed, and then sat down trembling and weeping.

Lisa did not go to the police. She did not speak of the incident to anyone. Rather, she waited for her husband Barry, who would return in two weeks from his current tour of duty in the Navy. Those two weeks were filled with fear for herself and her son. She had a great deal of self-doubt as to whether she had done the right thing, as well as considerable apprehension over how her husband would respond. Lisa knew that her rape was going to complicate an already stressful situation.

Others React

When her husband Barry finally returned home, he sensed almost immediately that Lisa was behaving in an unusual way. He asked her what was wrong. Not wanting to spoil Barry's homecoming, she claimed that everything was fine. However, her expression betrayed her words. Barry, never a particularly patient man, began to lose his temper and insisted that she tell him about the problem. Lisa could contain her tears no longer and blurted out that she had been raped.

Barry sat in stunned silence as Lisa recounted the event. He did not interrupt her but he clearly was becoming angry. When she finished, he said, "If I catch the b----, I'm going to kill him!" He told her that she shouldn't worry because he'd find a way to "get" the guy. He then proceeded to ask Lisa for information that would help him identify the rapist. "What did he look like?" "How tall was he?" "How old did he seem?" "What was he wearing?" "What did his voice sound like?" When Lisa claimed that she had no idea who the man was and appeared unable to provide Barry with answers, he became very annoyed with her and implied that she was being uncooperative. He never asked if she had seen a doctor of if she needed someone to talk to about the incident.

During the next several days, Barry appeared to be preoccupied with the rape and talked of it constantly. Not only was he deeply angered, he was also beginning to have doubts about Lisa's role in her victimization. He began to ask her questions such as, "Why didn't you lock the window?" "Why didn't you fight him?" "What do you think you did to make him pick you?" "Why did you decide not to call the police?" "Are you sure you don't have any idea who the guy is?" Even though this type of questioning upset Lisa very much, her husband seemed unable to contain his anger or doubts. He continued to make her discuss the incident.

Other aspects of their relationship also suffered. Barry spent little time with their son, preferring instead to be at the tavern "thinking." In terms of their sexual relationship, Lisa was confused and upset by what happened to her; she simply could not respond to Barry's advances. At first he appeared to be understanding and did not force the issue. Then one night after he had been drinking, Barry insisted that she "stop acting like a child and start acting like a wife." When Lisa apologized but still remained reluctant, Barry became abusive. He pushed her down and screamed at her, "If you can do it with him, you can do it with me!" Never did Lisa feel more alone than at that moment.

Barry was home for approximately six weeks before his next tour of duty. All the problems that existed in their marriage before Lisa's rape were exaggerated and brought out into the open. By the end of his stay, it was apparent that their marriage was in serious trouble. Lisa became aware of a fundamental failure in communication. She felt that Barry had abandoned her emotionally when she most needed him. For his part, the rape enhanced Barry's suspicions about Lisa's faithfulness. He could not understand why she seemed so cold and distant. In a way, the anger that each felt toward the rapist shifted toward the other person.

After Barry departed, Lisa and her son moved back to her parent's house. She is currently seeking the assistance of a counselor and is undecided about whether she is committed to continuing her marriage with Barry.

Lessons to be Learned

It is clear from Lisa's case that her husband's anger and distrust blinded Barry to her condition and to the problems she was facing. His initial preoccupation with revenge and his doubts about Lisa's judgment and fidelity only heightened her distress. Barry's drinking, his anger toward Lisa, and his premature demands that she be sexually responsive to his needs put severe strains upon their relationship. This prolonged her recovery and undermined the probabilities that their marriage would survive. It also reduced Barry's ability to function as a father, husband and lover. If Barry was to have played a positive role in Lisa's recovery, he should have acted much differently.

What Barry Should Have Done

- **Barry's first concern should have been Lisa's physical and mental welfare.** Barry should have insisted that his wife undergo a thorough medical examination. Not only would this have protected Lisa from disease and physical harm which may have resulted from the rape, it would also have been a demonstration of his love and support.

- **Barry should have put his anger and doubts aside, listened carefully to Lisa, and taken his cues from her.** Barry's quick interest in revenge was an indication that he was much more concerned with his own feelings than with those of his wife.

- **Barry should have refrained from "interrogating" Lisa.** In so doing, he would have greatly reduced her feelings of guilt and anxiety. Words of comfort and support were needed to assure Lisa that she was a victim; she was not in any way to blame for the rape.

- **Barry should have encouraged Lisa to seek the assistance of a counselor, perhaps at the nearest rape crisis center.** He should have also considered relationship counseling. Their marriage, which was in some jeopardy prior to the rape, was now in serious trouble. With professional help, communications between Barry and Lisa could have been improved.

- **Barry should not have intimidated Lisa into having sexual relations with him.**

By so doing, Barry demonstrated a lack of understanding and respect for the pain and terror Lisa experienced. His actions toward her communicated that he considered her to be a willing participant in a sexual act with a stranger—not a victim of violence. Barry should have realized that a woman who has been raped requires time to recover and to regain her normal desire for sexual intimacy. He should have been with Lisa to hold and comfort her—not to make sexual demands.

- **Barry should not have "abandoned" Lisa and their son.** In failing to spend time with his son, Barry placed the full responsibility of child care on Lisa. In addition, his absence from the home not only caused Lisa to worry, but also communicated his rejection of her and their son.

Case Study 4
Barbara: Rape Complicated by Racial Prejudice

The Incident

Barbara is a white, 45-year-old housewife who resides in a large city on the east coast. She and her husband Paul, a bus driver for the city transit system, have three children. Barbara does her grocery shopping every Tuesday morning at the same local supermarket where she has shopped for 13 years.

On this particular Tuesday, Barbara left the store with two armloads of groceries and walked around the side of the building to her automobile.

As she reached her car, two black men in their early twenties approached her and offered to help put the groceries in the trunk. Before she could reply, one of the men pulled out a knife and placed it to her throat while the other clamped a hand over her mouth and spun her around by the arm. As the groceries scattered in all directions, Barbara was dragged behind a dumpster and gagged with her own scarf. It was broad daylight and she could see houses across the street, but there were no people in sight. She was raped repeatedly by the two men and subjected to a stream of verbal abuse which left little doubt as to how the men felt about white females.

When the ordeal was finally over, the two rapists seemed surprisingly remorseful and were almost considerate. They helped her to her feet, brushed the dirt off her clothes, picked up the groceries on the ground beside her car and tossed them into the back seat. As soon as she was inside the car, she locked the doors and drove directly home. Once inside the garage, she began weeping.

Others React

She was still crying fifteen minutes later when her youngest son Tim, age 15, arrived home from school. He wanted to know what had happened. She simply told him to call the dispatcher at the transit company to request that her husband Paul be sent straight home. By the time Paul arrived, their daughter Karen, age 17, had also returned home from school. Barbara sent the children out of the room while she told the story to her husband. Paul called the police, who suggested that he take Barbara to the hospital immediately for an examination.

Two uniformed officers met them there to take a preliminary statement from Barbara.

Before leaving for the hospital Paul told the children: "Your mother has been raped by two black men. She's going to be all right, but she needs some medical attention. Then she has to talk to the police. I'll call you from the hospital. In the meantime, call your older brother at work and tell him what's happened." With that, Paul and Barbara left for the hospital.

Blake, the eldest son, left work at the foundry when his brother called. He drove to his parent's house to await the call from his father. As might be expected, Blake's younger siblings looked to him for guidance. When his father called home to recount what had happened, Blake went into an angry tirade about black people and "other low lifes who should be shot." He was convinced that the police and courts would probably do nothing about the crime and that the only way to guarantee justice was to "take it into your own hands."

For weeks after the rape, there seemed to be little progress in apprehending the rapists. Both Paul and Blake continually discussed, in front of the rest of the family, their feelings about black people who "live off the sweat of others, commit all the crimes, and still go free." These frequent expressions of outrage were beginning to have a profound impact on the others. For example, Karen became very reluctant to talk to one of her fellow high school cheerleaders who was black. She also felt very uneasy about black males at school, even though she had been on good terms with them all during high school.

Tim was also influenced by the racial sentiments of his father and older brother. He began to notice things about the blacks at school that had never before drawn his attention. He avoided sitting near blacks on the school bus and in the cafeteria. He and his friends found themselves frequently discussing how black people were "different" and how they always seemed to be the trouble makers at school. One day Tim and his friends vandalized several lockers used by black students. This in turn heightened racial tensions at school and set off several other interracial incidents. Tim and the others were caught and had to pay for damages. They also spent considerable time in detention. Although Tim's actions were frowned upon by school officials, at home his father and brother treated him like a hero.

As a consequence, Barbara was deeply affected not only by her victimization, but also by the perpetual discussions about blacks. Instead of the tension in the home subsiding during the weeks following the rape, it grew worse. Barbara became increasingly fearful that members of her family would end up hurt or in jail. She was especially upset over what happened to Tim at school. When she discovered that Blake had purchased a gun and was keeping it in his car, she was at a total loss as to what she could do. Finally, in order to protect Blake from himself, she removed the weapon from his car and threw it in the river. This made both her husband and Blake angry with her. The rapists were never caught but the subject of race continues to be an issue of contention in Barbara's family.

Lessons to be Learned

Due to her family's preoccupation with "racial justice," Barbara's recovery needs were poorly attended. Barbara's need for emotional support was shoved aside because of emotionally charged racial prejudices. As a result, the family became divided rather than united. Under no circumstances should Paul and Blake have been angry with Barbara for her actions concerning the gun. They needed to realize that her motive was to protect Blake from physical harm and legal entanglements. When family members take matters into their own hands, it is likely that they will make matters worse. They may even become targets of the legal system. This is a sure way to complicate the recovery of a rape victim.

Paul and Blake's reactions to the rape had an equally troubling impact on the younger children. Constant racial slurs and an interpretation of the rape strictly on the basis of race, made the children unduly fearful and angry toward all blacks. A generalized anxiety toward an entire group of people, based upon the assumption that they are all basically alike, is highly debilitating and an impediment to daily functioning. In the case of Karen, her previously friendly relationships with blacks suffered. In addition, her fear toward black males was developing into an unhealthy preoccupation. Such feelings probably would not have emerged if Paul and Blake had responded differently.

Also tragic is what happened to Tim. His actions grew out of the strong pressure for revenge against blacks that he felt at home. Certainly his beliefs about black people were based on inaccurate assumptions and tended to reflect the perpetual tensions of his home life. His actions in vandalizing the lockers at school only functioned to identify him as a trouble maker in the eyes of authorities. This had serious negative consequences for his subsequent academic performance. Unfortunately, Tim's father and older brother reinforced the very behavior which hurt both him and his mother.

In the final analysis, Barbara's recovery was complicated and prolonged by the behavior of Paul and Blake. She was made to assume the added burden of worrying about their safety, as well as the disturbing behaviors of the children. The atmosphere in the home caused by her husband and her elder son made it difficult for the family to function effectively. They were all hurt.

What Paul and Blake Should Have Done

- **Paul and Blake should have focused their attention upon Barbara's needs.** They should have left the issue of justice to the authorities. Because Paul and Blake were so caught up in seeking revenge, they neglected to provide the love and support which a rape victim desperately needs.

- **Paul and Blake should have realized that all men of any race are not rapists.** They should have communicated this to Barbara and the children. Such a generalization was very unfair and intensified existing racial prejudices. It also increased the family's anxiety and disrupted their lives.

- **Paul and Blake should have channeled their energy toward assisting in Bar-**

bara's recovery. They could have suggested professional counseling for Barbara. They could also have considered counseling for themselves to help them resolve their anger and frustration. This would have removed a large burden from Barbara, who became very concerned for her family's safety.

Case Study 5
Lori: Rape Victim with Supportive Partner

The Incident

Lori is an attractive 24-year-old woman who is employed as a distributor for a large textbook company. On an evening in March, Lori was returning to her apartment after a lengthy sales meeting. When she parked her car and opened the door a man appeared out of nowhere and grabbed her by the arm. He displayed a knife and forced her to drive with him to a deserted spot. He explained to her that they were going to "have some fun." If she screamed or in any way resisted, he would use the knife on her.

Although she did not suffer severe physical injury, Lori was subjected to extreme terror, vulgar language and degrading sexual acts. At no time during the rape did Lori feel she could effectively use force to resist the assault. However, she did plead with him (without success) to let her go. Even though the event seemed to her like a fragmented nightmare, Lori had the presence of mind to take mental notes that later proved helpful to the police.

After the attack, despite the fact that she felt "filthy," she went directly to the police without bathing or changing clothing. Lori was aware of the importance of physical evidence and was determined to see the rapist punished.

Others React

After a brief preliminary report, Lori was taken directly to a hospital for examination and treatment. Up until this point, Lori had remained remarkably controlled. However, it was at the hospital that she began to show signs of the emotional strain. This stress was further compounded by the actions of those who were supposed to help her. Lori was made to wait in the emergency room in her disheveled condition for nearly one hour. She was then examined by a male doctor. He was professional in demeanor, but did not appear to be sensitive to her emotional state. The series of rape examination procedures, though routine to the doctor, were discomforting to Lori and added to her distress. During this time, she was deeply concerned about the potential responses of her family and of John, her fiance, who as yet had not been informed of what happened.

When the medical examination had been completed, Lori was taken home by a police officer and allowed to bathe and change clothing. It was requested that she return to the police station that evening to provide a full account of the event. While at home, Lori telephoned her fiance to briefly explain what happened. She asked him to meet her at the police station. Although John was very upset and wanted her to explain more fully what had happened, he agreed to meet her as requested.

When John arrived at the police station, Lori was being questioned by detectives. As he sat waiting for her, John felt angry, hurt, confused, and highly apprehensive. He did not know what to expect. He was concerned about how this incident would change his relationship with Lori. As Lori emerged from the room where she was questioned, John held out his arms and they embraced without saying a word. Lori began to cry. Although John also felt like crying, he held her and told her how much he loved her. John wanted very much for Lori to tell him what happened, but he sensed that this was not the appropriate time for such a discussion.

When the police finished questioning her, John took Lori back to her apartment and offered to make her a hot meal. Although Lori seemed silent and distant, he realized that her silence was not an attempt to shut him out, but rather an understandable response to what had happened. It was then that John held her hand and said: "Look, I'm just as confused about this as you. I want to know what happened to you. However, I realize you may need some time to sort things out. Whenever you're ready, I'm willing to listen. I also want you to know that I don't blame you for what happened. You shouldn't blame yourself either. All that really matters is that you are okay; that we love each other. This is going to be hard on both of us but if we trust and help each other, I know we can get through it."

Lori was visibly relieved by what John said. However, she was very anxious about how her parents would react to news of the rape. John asked her if she would like him to break the news to her family. Together they discussed various approaches.

Lori decided that John would tell her family and, when she was ready, they would both answer any questions her parents had.

In part, as a result of his support and the support of her family, Lori decided to press charges against the rapist. The case was scheduled for trial and John was understanding and supportive of Lori's decision to pursue legal action. John took time off from work to be with her during the trial. They were married that fall.

Lessons to be Learned

John's behavior throughout Lori's ordeal suggests a high level of emotional security and self-awareness. John had no difficulty in understanding that she was a victim and therefore not responsible for what happened. He did not question her judgment nor her inability to physically resist the assault. Although he did have questions about what happened to her, he did not pressure her into talking about the incident. He took his cues from her rather than imposing his will by making decisions for her. John showed great patience and sensitivity by giving Lori's immediate needs a higher priority than his own.

Of equal importance to Lori's recovery, John communicated in clear terms that he did not hold her responsible for what occurred. He let her know that his love for her was unchanged. John also let her know that he was willing to help her and stick by her throughout the legal process. John's assistance in approaching Lori's family demonstrated his support. In a way, Lori's victimization dramatically proved John's love and trust. Their relationship was actually strengthened by the experience. Lori, as a result, was able to reclaim her health much sooner than is typical for many women following the horrid crime of rape.

What John Did

John clearly was an important asset in Lori's recovery. Husbands, fathers and male friends have much to offer recovering rape victims if they follow John's example.

- **John placed Lori's needs ahead of his own.** Because Lori was not distracted by John's struggles, she focused her full attention on her own feelings and recovery.

- **John provided support but followed Lori's cues.** While he offered advice, he allowed Lori to make her own decisions.

- **At no time did John suggest or imply that Lori was responsible for her victimization.**

- **John was helpful in communicating with Lori's family.** By doing so, he served as a buffer and further demonstrated his support for Lori.

- **John demonstrated his support for Lori by taking time off from work to be with her during the trial.**

- **Throughout the entire ordeal, John's presence and support assured Lori that she was not alone.** This was his greatest contribution.

Case Study 6
Ellen: Rape Victim with a Father Who Expressed His Anger Constructively

The Incident

It was Ellen's first visit to the large University attended by her older sister, Cynthia, and the directions to Cynthia's apartment—which Cynthia had dictated to her over the phone—were no help at all. Also, it was getting dark and the street signs were becoming more difficult to read. As she drove slowly along, looking for a phone booth, she saw two friendly-looking males standing next to their car. Given her proximity to the campus, she assumed that these males were students. Ellen stopped and asked them for directions to Cynthia's apartment. The men responded that they had a map in their car and she was welcome to look at it.

As she stood next to their car, studying the map in the deepening twilight, one of the men suddenly opened the back door of the car and the other man pushed her into it. Clamping his hand over her mouth to keep her from screaming, he whispered that if she kept quiet and cooperated, no harm would come to her. They then drove her to an apartment, where she was raped by both of them. Later, they dropped her off at a park several blocks from where her car was parked, and warned her: "Don't tell anyone about this. We have your driver's license, so we know where you live."

Still in a state of shock, Ellen nevertheless managed to get to a phone booth at a nearby convenience store and call Cynthia. Cynthia picked her up and drove her immediately to the university medical center emergency room. By the time the emergency room examination had been completed, Ellen had decided to go to the police station and file charges against her assailants. She did so and, later that night, she and Cynthia made a long distance call to their parents, Judy and Roger, to tell them what had happened. Roger had embarked recently on a second career as a counselor, and Ellen hoped that his newly-acquired crisis intervention skills would enable him to deal with what had happened.

Others React

Even though he knew that anger would not help his daughter recover, Roger was furious and could think of nothing but getting revenge against the "punks" who had violated Ellen. In a way, it was fortunate that Cynthia's apartment was a three hour drive from where they lived, because it gave Judy some time to help Roger vent his anger, *before* they met with Ellen. Judy, coincidentally, had been training as a volunteer at the local rape crisis center, and sooner than she expected, she was putting her training to use.

By the time they reached Cynthia's apartment, Roger had cooled down considerably. He hugged Ellen and told her that he loved her, that he and Judy were proud of her for having survived, and that they would be there to support her throughout the police investigation and subsequent trial.

On the way home, Judy told Roger that she was proud of *him*, too, for offering Ellen what she most needed. Roger confided that his intense hatred for the rapists had not gone away and wouldn't for a long time. To make matters worse, Ellen's case did not go to trial. Even though Ellen's case provided the prosecuting attorney with what Roger felt was clear-cut evidence of rape, the grand jury decided not to hand down an indictment against the assailants.

Confused and bitter, Roger nevertheless decided that "I should use my anger to solve problems, rather than create them." The following week, he began training as a volunteer at the local rape crisis center, in part to come to grips with his own emotions over what had happened to Ellen, but also to help other men who were "secondary victims" of sexual assault. He quickly discovered, however, that this particular rape crisis center's services were designed (as they should be) to help the primary victim, and that they were not able to offer him much help. He would have to seek assistance elsewhere. Also, from his own experience as a counselor, he knew that males are much less likely than females to seek help from counselors or other mental health professionals.

It was then that Roger decided to start a support group for male "significant others" of rape victims. He solicited referrals from the rape crisis center, the police, and the local community mental health center, and held the meetings in his own home. To his dismay, attendance at the meetings was (and still is) sporadic. Furthermore, he found that even in his group meetings, which were designed to be as non-threatening as possible, many of the men were still unwilling to open up and talk about what they were feeling. Nevertheless, several of the men remarked to Roger that the sessions had helped them through some very difficult emotional crises. In fact, a number of the participants indicated that this group was the only place where they felt that their feelings were understood and accepted, and that they were now able to deal more effectively with what had happened. Also, Roger was at last free of his anger and, consequently, his relationship with Ellen was better than it had ever been before.

Lessons to be Learned

In some respects, Roger's behavior was atypical in that he was not only willing to seek professional assistance immediately, but he also created an opportunity for other males to have an outlet for their feelings. Although he felt the same emotions as any loving father would under the circumstances, he was able to find a helpful rather than harmful way to deal with those powerful feelings. His chief concern was the recovery of his daughter, rather than finding a means to seek revenge. In the end, he created a family climate where all could recover, and where relationships were strengthened rather than tested to the limit.

What Roger Did

- **Roger found a constructive way to deal with his anger.** At no time did Roger let his desire for revenge override his judgment as to what was best for his daughter. He maintained enough emotional control and let her needs dictate his actions.

- **Roger consistently communicated a message of love and support to his daughter and to other family members.** In this manner, he helped create a nurturing climate for the recovery of each family member.

• **Roger set an example not only for his family, but for other males who have experienced the rape of a loved one.** By creating a support group for secondary victims, Roger was able to constructively deal with his feelings and allow others to do likewise. This represented a service beyond price.

Case Study 7
Nikki: A Victim of Drug-Facilitated Rape

The Incident

When she awoke on Sunday morning, Nikki was in a terrible state. Her head throbbed, her mouth tasted like cotton, and her body ached all over. Worst of all, she didn't know whose bed this was, how she had gotten here, or why she was naked from the waist down. As she gingerly raised herself to a sitting position and surveyed her surroundings, bits and pieces of the previous evening began to come back to her. She remembered leaving the basketball game with her friend Brent to go to a post-game party at the fraternity house, where one of Brent's fraternity brothers handed her a tall, sweet-tasting drink guaranteed, he said, to "pick you right up." Instead, the drink "laid her right down." The room started spinning, she felt flushed and disoriented, and she began to lose consciousness. The last person she saw before passing out was Brent, and she now realized that this was Brent's bedroom in the fraternity house, although Brent himself was nowhere to be found.

As she awakened completely and started piecing together the events of the preceding night, Nikki slowly began to realize what had happened. First of all, while not a heavy drinker, she had never been hammered like that by a single drink. Brent's friend, with or without Brent's knowledge, must have slipped something into her drink, maybe even one of the "date rape drugs" she had heard about in the dorm meetings at the beginning of the school year. Also, much of the soreness she was feeling was in the genital area, and it finally dawned on her that Brent had brought her to this room and assaulted her while she was passed out. That explained why she was only partially clothed, and why Brent was elsewhere!

Horrified, Nikki staggered to her feet, found her panties and jeans and put them on, and ran from the fraternity house to her room at the dorm. There, she quickly showered, dressed, and called her good friend Malcolm, who was the resident advisor (RA) for students living on this floor of the dorm. Even though Malcolm was a junior and Nikki was a freshman, the two of them had hit it off from the start, and he was the one person she felt she could trust.

Others React

As Nikki told her story, Malcolm was outwardly composed, but on the inside he was besieged by conflicting emotions: anger at Brent and his friend for what they had done to Nikki, and great sadness for what she must be going through. Then, he began to have questions, including:

- Why had she left the basketball game with Brent, whose reputation as a womanizer was well- known across campus?

- What was she doing at Brent's fraternity house, the same house where a coed had allegedly been drugged and assaulted last year?

- Having made the questionable decision to go to the fraternity house, why didn't she have a friend go with her?

- Given the stories circulating about this fraternity, why didn't Nikki guard against something being slipped into her drink. For instance, couldn't she make her own drink, or ask for a beer that she would open?

- Didn't Nikki realize that taking a shower this morning may have eliminated evidence needed to verify that she was sexually assaulted?

Despite his questions about Nikki's decision-making last night and this morning, Malcolm believed that she was telling the truth, and that communicating that belief to her was more important than getting answers to question that were troubling him. He suggested that Nikki phone one of the campus rape victim advocates, who could provide information she needed to decide what to do next.

After listening to Nikki's account, the advocate—Janet—suggested that she go immediately to the emergency room to make certain that she did not have any serious injuries, and offered to meet her there. Also, she asked if Nikki had a friend who would take her to the emergency room, and Malcolm said that he would.

At the hospital, the emergency room personnel carefully examined Nikki and, informed of the possible cause of her injuries, collected medical evidence that might be needed later. As they did so, Janet assured Nikki that the collection of such evidence did not commit her to filing a formal complaint.

On the way back to the dorm, Malcolm listened as Nikki listed her options, as outlined for her by Janet. Nikki realized that filing a complaint against Brent and his friend with the university's sexual assault hearing board would not make things easy for her. The members of the board, as well as others on campus, would ask tough questions about her behavior that night. She suspected also that before long, Brent's fraternity brothers would be suggesting that the "alleged assault" at their house was nothing more than a story concocted by a promiscuous coed who had consensual sex with one of the brothers and later regretted it.

Malcolm was familiar with this tactic; it had been used the previous year to discourage a female student from filing a complaint after an incident similar to this one. He agreed with Nikki that filing a complaint would take courage, but assured her that he—and her advocate—would support her whatever her decision.

In the end, Nikki decided that Brent and his friends had to be stopped, and she decided to file the complaint against Brent and the friend who had served her the drink. Later that semester, Nikki and the two men presented their versions of events to the hearing board. After lengthy deliberations, the board ruled that the men's behavior violated the university's code of conduct, and they were expelled. The men appealed, but the university administration upheld the decision. At the same time, the administration announced that the fraternity would be placed on probation, pending the outcome of an investigation into new allegations that other female students had been victims of drug-induced sexual assault.

Lessons to be Learned

In the aftermath of Nikki's horrific experience, Malcolm showed great sensitivity and presence of mind. Even though her recounting of events raised many questions, he believed her, and let her know that he believed her. Also, he understood that questioning her would imply that he held her at least partially responsible for what had happened, and he wisely refrained from doing so.

Equally valuable was Malcolm's RA training the previous summer, which alerted the RAs to the existence of the rape victim advocates and the services they could provide for sexual assault victims. Jane proved to be a sensitive, informed advocate, and after watching her skillful handling of the situation, Malcolm was grateful that she and the other trained advocates were available to the students.

Finally, Malcolm's promise to support her decision, whatever it turned out to be, showed Nikki that he trusted her to do what was best for her, and his quiet presence during the complaint board hearing assured her that she had a friend upon whom she could depend.

What Malcolm Did

In the midst of considerable emotional turmoil, Malcom was nevertheless able to step back from the situation and think clearly about what was best for Nikki.

Malcolm had questions about Nikki's decision-making that night, but refrained from asking them. A moment's reflection convinced Malcolm that asking such questions would serve no useful purpose, and would imply to Nikki that he thought her responsible for what had happened to her.

Malcolm's one and only suggestion was that Nikki contact one of the campus rape victim advocates. He was aware of a valuable campus resource, and quickly connected her with it. Then, he stepped back and allowed the advocate to do what she had been trained to do.

Malcolm offered unconditional support for whatever course of action Nikki chose. He felt strongly that Brent and the rest of his group needed to be punished for their actions, but understood that the decision to file a complaint could only come from Nikki. Also, he stood by her through the ordeal of the hearing, and as rumors about "who was really to blame" circulated around the campus.

Appendix B
Resources

American College of Obstetricians and Gynecologists
409 12th St., SW
Washington, DC 20024
Phone: (202) 638-5577
Website: www.acog.org

Centers for Disease Control and Prevention
National Center for Injury Prevention
Mailstop K65
4770 Buford Hwy., NE
Atlanta, GA 30341
Phone: (770) 488-1506
Website: www.cdc.gov/ncipc

Men Can Stop Rape
P.O. Box 57144
Washington, DC 20037-7144
Phone: (202) 265-6530

National Center for Victims of Crime
2111 Wilson Blvd., Suite 300
Arlington, VA 22201
Phone: (703) 276-2880
Website: www.ncvc.org

National Sexual Violence Resource Center
Pennsylvania Coalition Against Rape
125 N. Enola Dr.
Enola, PA 17025
Phone: (717) 728-9781
Website: www.nsvrc.org

National Organization for Victim Assistance (NOVA)
1757 Park Road, NW
Washington, DC 20010
Phone: (202)232-6682
Website: www.try-nova. org

Office for Victims of Crime Resource Center
Box 6000
Rockville, MD 20849
Phone: (800) 627-6872
Website: www.ncjrs.org

Rape Abuse & Incest National Network (RAINN)
252 10th St., NE
Washington, DC 20002
Phone: (800) 656-HOPE

U.S. Department of Justice
Office for Victims of Crime
810 7th St., NW
Washington, DC 20531
Phone: (202) 307-5983
Website: www.ojp.usdoj.gov/ovc